AFRIKAN FAMILY LEGACY MILLENNIUMS BEFORE SLAVERY

Tracing Tinsley Family MtDNA 140,000 B.C.E. To 1800 C.E.

ADETOKUNBO KNOWLES BORISHADE, Ph.D.

Published By

SANKOFA INTERNATIONAL PRESS
"Retrieving what has been lost"
Cleveland, Ohio

Sankofa International Press
"Retrieving what has been lost"
Cleveland, Ohio

Copyright © 2014 By
Adetokunbo Knowles Borishade

All rights reserved.
No part of this book may be reproduced in any form or by any means including electronic, mechanical, or photocopying or stored in a retrieval system without permission in writing from the publisher except by a reviewer who may quote brief passages to be included in a review.

Cover Design By Larry Tinsley

Interior Graphics By Adetokunbo K. Borishade

Library of Congress Catalog-in Publication Data

Borishade, Adetokunbo Knowles, Ph.D.
 Afrikan Family Legacy Milleniums Before Slavery: Tracing Tinsley Family MtDNA 140,000 B.C.E. to 1800 C.E.
Includes bibliographical references.

ISBN: 9780965400954 (Paperback)

1. Genealogy
2. Afrikan Migrations
3. Genetics
4. Afrikan History
5. Mitochondrial DNA
6. Afrikan Civilizations

PUBLICATIONS

Liberian Origins, Migrations, History and Destiny: Philosophical Speculations on Their Global Journeys as Bases for Inter-Ethnic Unity

Butting Heads: Testifying and Rescuing African Minds Worldwide with Traditional Yoruba Philosophy

Classical African Values and Yoruba Philosophy For African American Intervention and Personality Development

The Maafa Ritual of Healing, Remembrance, And Transcendance

Re-Aligning African Heads: Yoruba Curatives For Maafa-Related Ailments

AUDIOTAPE AND CD SERIES

African History & Culture Review: In the Groove:
Segment-1. "Africa: The Birthplace of Humanity"

Segment-2. "African Contributions to Philosophy, Religion, and Science"

Segment-3. "African Origins of Judaism, Christianity, And Islam"

Segment-4. "African Matriarchy and The Divine Feminine

PREORDINATION
Written By: Adetokunbo Knowles Borishade

You might brutalize us
With your cold wicked hands;
You might scatter us broadly
Throughout the lands;
You might utter blasphemies
None but you can comprehend;
But at the end of the day
We shall still unite, rise, and stand.

DEDICATION

This book is dedicated to my late maternal grandmother Elizabeth Tinsley of Fayette, Mississippi and to all family members who share her MtDNA haploid line before and after. I give honor to the entire line of grandmothers who came before her but whose names are unknown. We, the family, bless you for the blood that has been poured from living vessel to living vessel from the very beginning of humanity up to now. We praise you for life and for the opportunity to make this world a better place than we found it. We thank you for your waters of life in which we swam before ever experiencing the light of day, and for the rivers of brine shed from your eyes as you suffered to make a way for us.

I also dedicate the book to my Aunt Omelia Tinsley Beverly who early on positively impacted my young life more than she can imagine.

Ase, ase, ase-ooo!

Adetokunbo Knowles Borishade
AKA Evelyn Louise Knowles

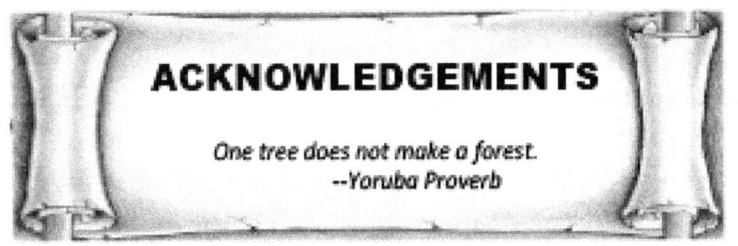

ACKNOWLEDGEMENTS

One tree does not make a forest.
--Yoruba Proverb

Appreciation is extended to my family, because this book would not have been written if not for their strong, loving encouragement and assistance. I undertook this project inspired by the wisdom of Booker T. Washington, who in 1895 admonished Afrikan Americans to "cast down your buckets where you are." I spent so many consecutive years as an educator in Africa making contributions to our people there. Once I returned home to Cleveland, Ohio in 2013 my first thought concerned how to use my education, training, research, and experiences to uplift my own family first, then my extended community family and world family after them.

The Tinsleys of Cleveland, Detroit, and Chicago decided on the theme *"Celebration of Life and Ancestry"* for the 2013 Family Reunion. It was as if the Ancestors were speaking to us, nudging and urging us in the right direction. That was when I informed the family of the MtDNA laboratory test that I had done back in 2007. The family consensus was to establish the 2013 celebration as the "Family Tree Project-1," signifying that there would be further developments in subsequent years. We had a 45-minute workshop during the 2013 Reunion, during which I presented historical narratives based upon the genetic laboratory report. Attendees each received a copy of the 7-page document that I was barely able to squeeze out in time for the event. As non-attendees heard about the Project and the document, they requested copies which were sent out later by email. After the Reunion, family members immediately organized themselves on one of the social mediums. The momentum of their communication, research, and participation increased over the following months. Therefore, I am grateful to the family that this modest publication became a reality.

The book is the result of conducting online research that further develops the original 7-page document. The book coordinates the genetic laboratory base data with historical, cultural, and archaeological data. Thus, the book first genetically traces our ancient grandmothers' journeys from the time they walked out of Afrika around 140,000 B.C.E. and began to help populate the Earth, along with some other Afrikan MtDNA haploid groups.

The Genebase Laboratory study revealed that the Afrikan Tinsley MtDNA haploid group is found among the Mbundu people of Angola, West Afrika. At that point the book presents a brief history of our ancestors' activities in Angola between 1200 and 1600 C.E. Explanation is given as to how Mbundu people were brought into the Virginia colony of America during the Afrikan Slave Trade.

Finally, the book reveals the economic dynamics that motivated Caucasian Tinsleys to join the "Great White Planter Migration" out of Virginia into Mississippi and other newly developing states in the Deep South, forcibly carrying their Afrikan slaves with them.

Many thanks to my niece Zena Tate, and my cousin Patreece Snell for their editing help. Their sharply pointed critical comments made significant improvements to the reading. Their assistance made it possible to publish this book on schedule in time for the August 2014 Reunion.

Thanks also to my cousin Larry Tinsley, the brilliant artist who designed the fertility doll image on the book cover. I recently met Larry, although he has been living in Cleveland all these many years. I attribute our meeting, at this very pregnant period of the family's sense of collective history, to the guiding hands of God and Grandmother Tinsley.

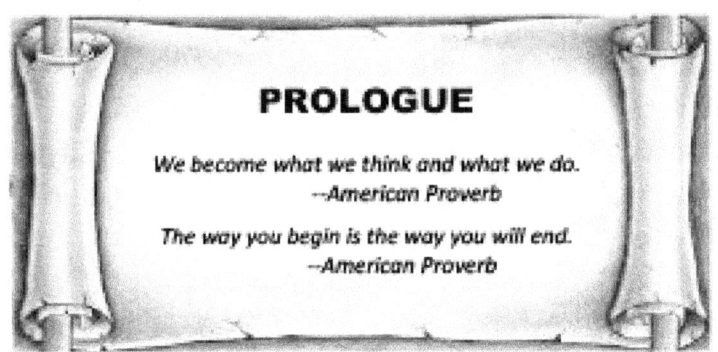

PROLOGUE

We become what we think and what we do.
--American Proverb

The way you begin is the way you will end.
--American Proverb

As I was putting the final touches on this book my mind went back to a previous one published in 2007 entitled *"Butting Heads."* In the Foreword of that book I spoke of how my spirit grieved because of the ongoing social decline in Afrikan American society. The decline is due to our failure to teach Afrikan history and culture to our children at home and in the education system. I left America to teach at an Afrikan university in 2008 and returned home in 2013. Imagine my dismay and sense of cultural shock to find the situation even worse. Our teenagers and young adults are suffering a loss of spirituality, pro-social values, and cultural norms; the very qualities that separate human beings from many of the lower animals.

We cannot blame the children and youths because they are the victims who have been subjected to several generations of parental ignorance of **the real Afrikan history and culture**. As far back as the late 1960s and early 1970s Black folks in America stepped into the trap of accepting **assimilation** as a necessary component of **integration**. Assimilation is an anthropology term which describes the manner in which people in one society reject their own culture and adopt the culture of a different group. This has spelled suicide for Afrikan Americans because it has resulted in losing the beliefs, values, historical wisdom, sense of identity, patterns of living, ways of organizing ourselves, and appropriate ways of responding to everyday challenges that ensure advancement and autonomy.

The losses and social decline are now so great that to a large extent our children are losing their sense of humanity in very real terms. To put it succinctly, Afrikan Americans have adopted the four defining features of Western culture: racism, sexism, imperialism, and hegemony (cultural imposition). In other words, too many of us now believe in White supremacy and all it entails. This radical assimilation results in being under attack from inside one's own psyche, as well as from a hostile society. Once you are mentally and psychologically against yourself, there is no way to survive, let alone achieve advancement and autonomy.

One's first instinct might be to challenge even the suggestion that human beings can lose their humanity. After all, didn't Almighty God create us as humans in a likeness with the Divine? Is it at all possible to lose one's humanity? The answers to both questions are: yes, and yes. If we say with conviction that Almighty God created the Universe and all that is within it, then **God is the Ultimate Scientist** and the original designer-creator of the process we refer to as **evolution**.

That being said, it should be an easy stretch to accept Almighty Creator God as the One who designed the evolutionary development of what is now the three-part human brain. If we begin to examine that three-part, interactive structure of the human brain within the context of behavior, we may be shocked to realize it is possible to lose one's humanity by functioning on a sub-human level. Only by allowing oneself to be dominated by the neocortex can someone function as a human being who is spiritually evolved and fit for society. Such a proposition appears harsh and outrageous at first, but might deserve some reflection and discussion.

Doctors and nurses all know that the human brain is constructed of three distinct parts: the reptile brain; the mammal brain; and the neocortex. The **reptile brain** first appeared in cold-blooded fish almost 500 million years ago, and it is the oldest of the three brain structures. Its highest expression was in cold-blooded reptiles around 250 million years ago. This ancient brain structure makes up the **brain stem** and the **cerebellum**. It is rigid, compulsive, and focused only on survival. This structure motivates a "cold-blooded" mindset and behavior that can kill without emotion. (Adapted from: (http://thebrain.mcgill.ca/flash/d/d_05/d_05_cr/d_05_cr_her/d_05_cr_her.html).

The **mammal brain** is called the **limbic system**, and it developed as an add-on located on top of the reptile brain. It first appeared in warm-blooded mammals about 150 million years ago. The mammal brain is responsible for emotions and empathy. Within its main structures are the hippocampus, the amygdala, and hypothalamus. The limbic system or mammal brain is the seat of the human conscience. It allows the formation of value judgments and decision making. This part of the brain has a strong influence on behavior by recording memories of behaviors that produce agreeable and disagreeable experiences. In other words, it enables an ability to learn from past experiences. (Adapted from: (http://thebrain.mcgill.ca/flash/d/d_05/d_05_cr/d_05_cr_her/d_05_cr_her.html).

The **neocortex** is situated on top of the mammal brain. This structure is a further add-on which developed in primates only about 2 or 3 million years ago as Homo sapiens began to emerge. It is separated into two large cerebral hemispheres; one on the right and one on the left. The neocortex is responsible for the development of human language, abstract thought, imagination, higher consciousness, spirituality, and culture. It is very flexible and has almost infinite learning abilities. This structure of the human brain is designed to be the executive control center of the human brain. However, the human will comes into play as individuals make choices in life. The more neocortex dominance is developed, the higher an individual functions or behaves as a human being. (Adapted from: (http://thebrain.mcgill.ca/flash/d/d_05/d_05_cr/d_05_cr_her/d_05_cr_her.html).

As we witness the behavior of many young Afrikan Americans <u>within the context of American society in general</u>, the critical questions deal with which structure of the human brain dominates the behavior of some people. We are witnessing a sharp increase in senseless, emotionless homicidal violence, which is greatly assisted by drug abuse and gun ownership. This is an indication that <u>*some persons are dominated by their subhuman reptile brain*</u>.

Since the arrival of Europeans into the New World, Afrikan Americans and Native Americans have been brutally familiar with reptile brain fixation. Meanness, violence, selfishness, radical materialism, limitless greed, lack of control, lack of compassion and empathy, and a lack of conscience in wrongdoing defines a people who are dominated and driven by their cold-blooded reptile brain. Such persons choose to relinquish the humanizing qualities and capabilities provided by the neocortex. Instead, their conscious behavioral choices reduce them to the same level as the cold-blooded fish, lizard, snake, turtle, frog, etc.

Up until the 1970s Afrikan Americans held on to our humanity in the face of brutal inhumanity towards us. Today that Afrikan sense of humanity is on a slippery downward slope. We must continue to *e-volve* into spiritually higher beings with higher intelligence; people with morality who perform higher-level thinking; people who make the world a better place; people who overcome grievous adversity by our spirituality and the strength of our character. A dangerously large number of us are *de*-**volving** into unfeeling sub-humans who are capable of destroying others without remorse. We are developing a critical mass of people who are adopting the same mindset and behaviors that define a huge segment of the larger American society; behaviors which we have historically detested and fought against.

Afrikan people must come to ourselves, remember who we once were, and return to the glory that is not only our historical legacy, but our God-given birthright. Most people of Afrikan descent don't realize that ancient history is Afrikan history, and that the glorious accomplishments of ancient civilizations were made by Afrikans. They don't know that Afrikans are the parents of all humanity. They are unaware that Afrikans had already built pyramids and created agriculture, science, mathematics, physics, astronomy, medicine, embalming, and much more when the rest of humanity throughout Eurasia were stuck in the Ice Age. It was our Afrikan ancestors who pitied them enough to travel into Eurasia and lift them out of Stone Age barbarity. It was Afrikans who gifted everything to world civilizations that they now claim for themselves. Those world civilizations now feel they no longer need to show gratitude to those who gave them so much from their beginning.

I maintain that for people of Afrikan descent everywhere, the combination of Afrikan history and culture is like the stone that the builders rejected. The house we are attempting to build does not and will not stand without this chief cornerstone.

That being said, I return to the reason for writing this book. Self-knowledge is the only sure way to develop self-esteem, positive self-image, self-pride, self-compassion, and a positive self-concept. It is hoped that the genetic-historical-archaeological approach that I used to trace my family genealogy through the annals of human history will inspire other families to do the same. In this way we can get down to the business of **creating positive change in ourselves and our children**, rather than wasting time trying to change others.

Our behavior is similar to the behavior of someone suffering the Battered Wife Syndrome. The battered wife is always seeking to change her spouse, when it is she who desperately needs to change herself. When we change ourselves, everything else has to change in response. Our future advancement and autonomy as human beings who are the parents of all humanity and the original bringers of world civilization depend on that change. We must return to our former selves and take charge of saving not only ourselves, but this world as well.

Adetokunbo K. Borishade, Ph.D.

LIST OF FIGURES

Chapter   **Page**

FIGURE-1:
MtDNA Test Certificate............................ 4

FIGURE-2
How MtDNA Is Passed On By Females.. 7

FIGURE-3
DNA map showing 200,000 years of haplogroup migrations............................ 38

TABLE OF CONTENTS

	Page
INTRODUCTION	1

CHAPTER-1
OUR ANCIENT MOTHERS: MTDNA and "MITOCHONDRIAL EVE".............. 23

CHAPTER-2
AFRIKAN TINSLEY FAMILY MTDNA MUTATIONS AND MIGRATIONS.............. 33

CHAPTER-3
AFRIKAN TINSLEY PREHISTORIC HUMAN DEVELOPMENT.............. 41

CHAPTER-4
AFRIKAN TINSLEY CULTURAL ACCOMPLISHMENTS.............. 71

CHAPTER-5
AFRIKAN TINSLEYS: FROM ANGOLA TO VIRGINIA.............. 89

CHAPTER-6
CAUCASIAN TINSLEYS: FROM ENGLAND
TO VIRGINIA TO MISSISSIPPI...................... 101

CHAPTER-7
CONCLUSION... 109

REFERENCES.. 113

ONLINE TOPICAL REFERENCE
SOURCES.. 113

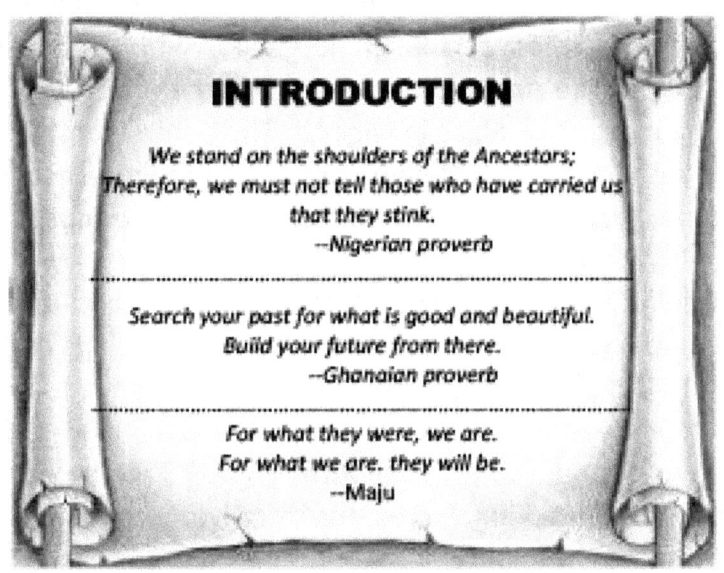

This informal study coordinates and records genetic, cultural, archaeological, and historical lineage of all relatives who are included in my MtDNA haplogroups ("L: M/CZ/D") in my mother's line. A haplogroup is a group of people who share the same ancestor on either the maternal or paternal line. Each haplogroup is assigned a letter.

In particular, these are the genetic groupings found to be part of Elizabeth Tinsley's mitochondrial DNA (MtDNA). Elizabeth Tinsley is the maternal grandmother of this author Evelyn Louise Knowles of Cleveland, Ohio, who legally adopted the traditional Afrikan name given by Yoruba traditionalists in Nigeria. The name literally means: Ade(*The Crown*)-tokunbo(*has returned home from a great distance*); **A**(*She brings*)-borishade(*the power of God and the Angels/Orishas with her*). I have tried my best to live up to that name which carries the blessings of both Almighty God and the ancestors.

Grandmother Elizabeth Tinsley's name is used as a unifying factor and a rallying point for what has become an ongoing "Family Tree Project" that began during the 2013 Family Reunion in Cleveland, Ohio. The annual Project now involves continuing the genealogical research where this book leaves off. The term "Afrikan Tinsley" is used to differentiate between the Caucasian Tinsley planters and my Afrikan ancestors who adopted or were given the surname of their plantation owners. It is understood that some contemporary Afrikan Tinsleys may be related by blood or by association of having ancestral roots on Caucasian Tinsley plantations throughout the South.

It needs to be made clear that although this document relates to the Afrikan Tinsley family in particular, the book's relevance does not end there. It generally relates to all persons of Afrikan descent who are not knowledgeable about the true history of our people that was written out of world literature 500 years ago. Using an even broader perspective, the book indirectly alludes to all the other Afrikan and non-Afrikan haploid chromosome groups in the world. All human ancestors began with the one solitary Afrikan haploid family group "L"; the group from which all humanity sprang forth. Other haploid groups developed as a result of various mutations as people migrated out of Sudan in northeast Afrika, branched off in various directions, and settled in different locations across the face of the Earth. Some of those groups changed physically into so-called "races" because they settled permanently in climates that were colder than tropical Afrika.

I had the MtDNA test conducted in the latter part of 2007, shortly before leaving the United States for a university teaching contract in Afrika in 2008. The laboratory mailed me the kit containing two large Q-tips with a set of instructions. I swabbed the inside of my mouth with them, sealed them in the protective envelope, and mailed them in. Two months later I received the test results along with some very specific printed information, a certificate, a haploid migration map, and an open account that lets me interact with others around the world who share the same MtDNA haploid line. **Figure-1** is the MtDNA Certificate I received from the Genebase Laboratory.

FIGURE-1
MtDNA Test Certificate

The DNA Ancestry Project

Certificate of Mitochondrial DNA Testing for Genetic Genealogy

Based on PCR testing in the mtDNA, we hereby certify that sample of

Adetokunbo Borishade

differs from the Cambridge Reference Sequence (CRS) at the following sequence locations in HVR-1 (16001 - 16520):

Location	Mutation Type	Nucleotide Change
16223	Substitution	C > t
16265	Substitution	A > t
16519	Substitution	T > c

Hyper Variable Region 1 (HVR-1) for Adetokunbo Borishade

Provided By Genebase Labratories. www.Genebase.com

It wasn't until I returned home in 2013 that any thought occurred of utilizing it as an educational tool. When I consulted the family about using the Mitochondrial DNA (MtDNA) laboratory results as the centerpiece of the family reunion this year and each year afterward, they joyfully agreed. My family literally jumped on the idea, and they chose the title "Celebration of Life and Ancestry" as our ongoing Family Tree Project theme.

Genebase Laboratory results became the basis of a seven-page document prepared for the family in August 2013. That small document in turn developed into this Study. The Genebase Laboratory report begins with 140,000 B.C.E.[1]; however, I have presented 200,000 B.C.E. as a starting point, based on my prior published research findings. From that point I followed the laboratory's findings on my family's MtDNA haploid migration paths and began to trace their journeys throughout history. I chose my mother's haploid MtDNA line to be tested because a female's bloodline is continuous throughout time.

---

[1] B.C.E. stands for "Before the Current Era," which is more acceptable to non-Christians. It replaces B.C., which means "Before (the birth of) Christ."

Going through the male YDNA line cannot provide the same result because YDNA is discontinuous over time.

MtDNA is structurally different from the linear, winding double-helix nuclear DNA found in the nucleus of the cell that most people are familiar with. MtDNA appears as a round circle, called a "plasmid." Nuclear DNA is 49,530,000 to 247,200,000 bases in length, compared with MtDNA, which is only approximately 16,569 to 16,571 in length. (Retrieved from www,genebase .com).

MtDNA is passed down from a mother to both her male and female offspring, but only female offspring have the capacity to pass it on to successive generations. **(See FIGURE-2)** Thus, as long as the females in an MtDNA line give birth to females in an unbroken succession up to now, they can be traced back some 140,000 years. As mentioned earlier, I chose the Afrikan Tinsley family name for this study in order to include as many extended family members as possible within the genetic parameters of the laboratory findings. In essence, this book commemorates the name of my maternal grandmother Elizabeth Tinsley.

Scientists speculate on the various factors that led Afrikan Tinsley pre-historic females to leave their Afrikan homeland in the Sudan. Drought, curiosity, adventure, and more plentiful food sources may be some of the motivations that caused them to embark on such ventures.

FIGURE-2
How MtDNA Is Passed On By Females

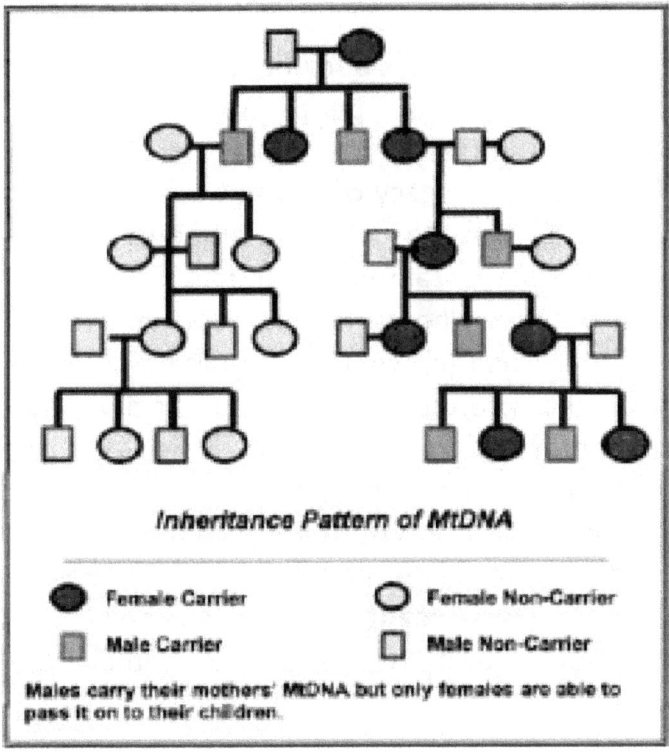

Inheritance Pattern of MtDNA

- ● Female Carrier
- ○ Female Non-Carrier
- ■ Male Carrier
- □ Male Non-Carrier

Males carry their mothers' MtDNA but only females are able to pass it on to their children.

Whatever the reasons for migration were, the laboratory results provided genetic evidence of their journeys over the millennia that made this publication possible. Genebase Laboratory test results reveal how Afrikan Tinsley ancient ancestors played a major role in the evolution of modern human beings. Together with several other dominant bloodlines, they were responsible for populating and colonizing the entire world.

The power of this document lies in knowing that whatever a group of people have done before can be repeated. Therefore, this record of Afrikan Tinsley ancestors' legacy of brilliant achievements and contributions to world civilization lays a foundation for several things: (a) who we are as a family group; (b) who we should be as individuals in this family; and (c) what we should be doing to carry on the splendid legacy of our ancient and more contemporary ancestors. However, the implications reach far beyond the Afrikan Tinsley family because the information refers to the ancestral legacies of ALL people of Afrikan descent whose ancestors made similar journeys and contributions during many of the same time periods.

Methodology

A simple, straightforward method was used in preparing this publication. Once I submitted my sample to Genebase Laboratories they ran the test along my mother's line and sent me the base data with information on my MtDNA haplogroup. The laboratory also provided me with a map which shows the migration paths taken by my ancient grandmothers on their journeys from 140,000 years ago when they first walked out of Sudan and began to populate the world. Genebase Laboratories further provided dates for the origin of worldwide civilizations that my ancient grandmothers helped to start as a result of settling and populating those lands. In addition, the MtDNA test identified the Mbundu people of Angola as my tribe of origin.

I compiled and presented the research in the name of my maternal grandmother Elizabeth Tinsley in order to attract and attach the various "branches" of the family to Grandmother's ancient African "roots" as well as to her "tree." It was assumed that the surname Tinsley was the "adopted" name of the plantation owner after Afrikan names were taken away. This was a common practice among both enslaved and freed

Africans, especially after Reconstruction when Afrikans' possession of a surname was necessary for public records.

My approach was first to coordinate the base data with archaeological, historical, and cultural information to "flesh out" the genetic data. I began to research all of the civilizations indicated in the base data as having been established by women and men in my MtDNA haplogroup from 140,000 B.C.E. forward. Once this was completed I presented the historical background of the Mbundu people of Angola from 1200 to 1619 C.E., the time when they were first captured and brought to the colony of Virginia.

Grandmother's maiden name was used to locate the African Tinsleys in Virginia. They were found by following the activities, movements, and genealogy of the White planter Thomas Tinsley, who immigrated into Virginia from England in 1638. A brief history of Virginia was included as a means of noting what slavery was like in the colony between 1600 and 1800. By searching public records the Caucasian Tinsleys were further studied to discover how Grandmother and other African Tinsleys got from Virginia to Mississippi and other southern states. In the process, both public records and historical accounts informed of a general dispersal of White planters from Virginia into other Deep Southern states such as Louisiana, Arkansas, Louisiana, Tennessee, Georgia, as well as Mississippi. Tinsley plantation owners were among them, and like other White planters, they forcibly carried their slaves with them.

Purposes

The primary purpose for preparing this combined genetic, archaeological, and historical record is to push back against the highly organized, systematic, collective assault on Afrikan psyches worldwide that has been waged for more than 500 years. This collective assault has been carried out in every institution of society, including religion. The assault continues worldwide and is not minimized by stories of individual success and achievement that are often narrated as a means of creating confusion and diversion from the truth. In fact, the more successful the Afrikan individual becomes, the greater the assault brought against her or him. The race-based political tribulations presently experienced by the Obama presidency are vivid, living evidence of this.

I also aim to inspire the children and youths in my blood family and my world family to strive for excellence and mastery in this world. The young ones desperately need this positive information imprinted in their minds to provide an irrefutable alternative image about themselves and our people as a whole. The narratives within this document can form a new, **evidence-based mental template** about how Afrikan ancestors were a distinct group of people on this Earth who accomplished great things for all humanity and civilization.

Another purpose for preparing this publication is to inspire a spirit of intellectual and academic inquiry such that our children will be motivated not only to value education and learning in general, but also to study the racial accomplishments of our Afrikan ancestors. This book is intentionally documented with online citations so that anyone with internet access will be able to conduct casual research on their own to gain further information and verification about the contents of this book.

A final purpose for this study is to present an alternative to the Biblical genealogy of the

Hebrews/Jews, which only goes back to about 6,000 years ago. That is the starting point for when they began as a distinct ethnic group. Hebrews are not the first or the original ethnic group of this Earth, their civilization is not the first to develop in the world, and their history becomes pale and watery when compared to Afrikan/Nubian genealogy and worldwide accomplishments.[2]

Throughout the world we have been taught to admire and valorize the accomplishments of every cultural and racial group except our own. We have been taught that every racial and ethnic group in the world has made contributions to civilization and to humanity except Afrikans, when nothing can be farther from the truth. Afrikan ancestors walked this Earth for tens of thousands of years when there was no one except them. Afrikan ancestors successfully brought all humanity through millions of years of an exceedingly long evolutionary period. Afrikans are the parents of all humanity, proven by the fact

---

[2] Evidence demonstrates that Nubian civilization and culture were the first to develop on Earth. We are now learning that the ancient Hebrews were actually Afrikans. Nevertheless, as landless nomads Hebrews developed as a distinct ethnic group thousands of years after Nubians.

that only Afrikan women contain the genetic makeup in their MtDNA of every human being on Earth. No other females have the "full package." (Retrieved from http://www.genebase.com/learning/article/17).

Genetic evidence helps us to understand that as Afrikan ancestors walked out of tropical Afrika into colder regions of the world, the women's highly complex MtDNA had the ability to mutate and produce offspring with physical features and characteristics which allowed for survival in colder and even arctic climates.

Archaeological evidence demonstrates that Afrika is the first Cradle of Civilization. Our Afrikan ancestors had already developed the first systems of religion, writing, calculation, mathematics, physics, astronomy, agriculture, medicine, surgery, architecture, irrigation, pyramid building, and more when the Semitic peoples were still nomadic and semi-nomadic desert dwellers living in tents. Similarly, Caucasians were still stuck in a Stone Age culture within an Ice Age environment. Both were far behind the reality of Afrikan civilization at the time.

Those who wish to have us remain blind to the facts of Afrikan achievement have convinced the world that the ancient Hebrews were Caucasians, and their racist version of Biblical mythology should be our only reality. The political and religious status quo find it highly problematic that Afrika was the place where humanity and civilization began because of prevailing racist historical, cultural, and religious teachings that have been imposed upon the world for centuries. These teachings have been imposed for so long that masses of Afrikans and non-Afrikans now believe them.

Some fundamental Christians have been led to believe that belief in science is somehow against belief in Almighty God. This is against the whole understanding of why Almighty God gave human beings a brain to be used. As an ordained minister for some 35 years, and as an Assistant Pastor, I hold the view that Almighty God is the ultimate scientist, evidenced by the wondrous, orderly working of the universe. Therefore, the more I learn about science, genetics, mathematics, nature and astronomy, the more I believe in the miraculous awesomeness of a Creator God who freely created this universe.

People usually engage in two types of narrative in this regard: (a) the narrative of faith, which relies upon subjective religious beliefs; and (b) the narrative of fact, which is based upon objective physical evidence. However, religion and science alike involve both subjective and objective elements in their search for truth and reality. In my opinion, then, belief in God and belief in science are not fundamentally incompatible, are not polar opposites, and are not in conflict with each other. Each one simply involves a different valid approach to reality.

We know that whatever is taught to a child from birth to six years of age will remain in that child's mind for a lifetime. Therefore, it is strongly suggested that the types of narratives presented in this document should be read to Afrikan children and youths in every generation as often as possible. If this is done those children will know that greatness is their birthright and contribution to humanity and civilization is their responsibility. They will know without a doubt, and will be able to prove with scientific and spiritual certainty, that they are God's original model for humanity. More importantly, they will also understand that those to whom much has been given, much is also expected in return.

Limitations

The documentation presented in this book is limited to Internet sources. As such, it does not pretend to be a product of strictly formal research. Another limitation involves the book's timeline. The family history-genealogy is presented from 200,000 B.C.E. up to 1800 C.E.[3]. Around 1600 C.E. is the time when Afrikan Tinsley ancestors belonging to the Mbundu Tribe of Angola were captured and transported into the western hemisphere. This tribal information was also provided by Genebase Laboratory results. Most Afrikan captives were first sent to Central and South America to be "seasoned" prior to being sent to American colonies like Virginia. "Seasoning" was the process of torturing and abusing Afrikan captives until they submitted to the reality of their slave status.

The study intentionally stops at 1800 C.E. in the expectation that younger relatives will be

---

[3] C.E. refers to "Current Era," and replaces A.D. "Anno Domini" — Latin for "The Year of Our Lord." In other words, A.D. refers to the **birth** of Jesus Christ and does not mean "After Death."

motivated to conduct the family research from that time forward. I leave it to them to collect and record Afrikan Tinsley family history from 1800 C.E. until now. The records, anecdotes, and experiences of our family throughout American history need to be gathered from our elderly members. It is critical that they record what the elders remember, especially the accomplishments. Of equal importance are the stories and experiences during periods of slavery and lynching; Reconstruction; Jim Crow; the migration into southwestern and northern states; the Harlem Renaissance; the race riots of 1919, 1943, and the 1960s; World War I; World War II; Korean War; Viet Nam War; War in Iraq; etc.

Chapter 1 presents a layman's explanation of mitochondrial DNA and its central importance in tracing the genealogy of living humans today according to the prevailing "Out-of-Afrika" theory. It also relates why genetic scientists refer to the first mother of all humanity as "Afrikan Eve," which is reminiscent of the biblical Eve, but is not the same as the Eve in biblical mythology.

Chapter 2 explains and outlines results of the laboratory MtDNA test upon which this short family-related study is based. The test results demonstrate the naturally-occurring blood mutations (changes) that occurred for hundreds of millennia[4], along with the migration routes of ancient Afrikan Tinsley females from 200,000 B.C.E. to 1600 C.E. The Chapter also briefly discusses the theoretical framework within which MtDNA genebase research is conducted.

Chapter 3 charts the global history and cultural development of Afrikan Tinsley ancestors during pre-historic times by following the base data provided by the Genebase Laboratory. This Chapter includes the evolutionary development of modern humans from the time they left the Afrikan homeland about 140,000 B.C.E., to consequently populate and colonize the entire Earth.

Chapter 4 details the Afrikan Tinsley ancestors' cultural accomplishments and contributions to human civilization from the time of recorded history, about 3300 B.C.E. to 1200 C.E. The Genebase test results provide data that trace

---

[4] A millennium = 1,000 years, while 2,000 or more years are expressed as "millenniums" (Engl) or "millennia," (Lat) in the plural forms.

Afrikan Tinsley MtDNA right up to the coast of West Afrika during the time of the Transatlantic slave trade.

Chapter 5 features the relationship that existed between the people of Angola and the Kongo during the Afrikan slave trade. Genebase laboratory data reveal that the Afrikan Tinsley haploid group today is found predominantly among the people of Angola, with small traces found among the contemporary people of the Kongo. This Chapter explains the historical connection between groups in these two nations. The chapter also presents the historical background as to how Afrikan Tinsleys were forcibly taken from Angola and brought into the Virginia colony around the 1600s. According to American historical records Virginia was the first colony to admit Afrikans as indentured servants and slaves in 1619. This chapter briefly explains the socio-political environment of Virginia in the 1600s-1700s. It also discusses how Afrikans went from being indentured servants to perpetual slaves generation after generation.

Chapter 6. It is well known that Afrikan Americans took on the surnames of their slave masters. This practice was especially necessary after Reconstruction when public records required both a first and last name. This chapter provides more information about what happened to Grandmother Elizabeth's Angola ancestors in Virginia by examining the Caucasian Tinsley family history. The genealogy of Thomas Tinsley records his activities from the time he left England to begin a new life in the American colonies. This man was the progenitor of all the Caucasian Tinsleys in America. By following the life history of Thomas Tinsley, along with census records, it was possible to validate that Afrikan Tinsleys were taken from Virginia into Mississippi and other states in the Deep South, along with their slave owners.

Chapter 7 concludes with notes of encouragement to Afrikan World families to create similar studies based upon their MtDNA test results. Doing so, and teaching their children the narratives from the studies, has the power to change history by changing ourselves from the inside out.

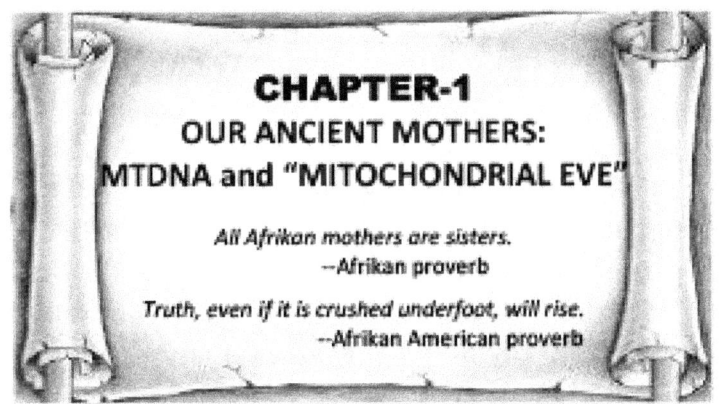

CHAPTER-1
OUR ANCIENT MOTHERS:
MTDNA and "MITOCHONDRIAL EVE"

All Afrikan mothers are sisters.
--Afrikan proverb

Truth, even if it is crushed underfoot, will rise.
--Afrikan American proverb

Today's genetic science reveals that there is only one species of human beings. The scientific findings of genetic research undermine the entire concept of different "races" or sub-species of humanity. The field of genetics has proven that by tracing human ancestry through mitochondrial DNA (MtDNA).

Racism and the plan to bring all people of color and their resources under Caucasian domination is the reason why this information has been removed from history and kept hidden for hundreds of years. Scientific studies demonstrate that Caucasians have fabricated a false history about themselves. Since truthful alternative information has been suppressed for so long, masses of Africans and non-Afrikans have come to believe that what they have been taught is true.

We must understand that there are at least two different ways of lying: by *com*mission and by *o*mission. Lying by *commission* is done by outright not telling the truth. The other is by *omission*, which means someone knows the truth but refuses to tell it. In a court of law, the latter is treated the same as the former. Thus, Malcolm X was 100 percent correct in his speech entitled "The Ballot or the Bullet": *"You've been had. You've been took. You've been hoodwinked. Bamboozled. Led astray. Run amok!"*

While the entire world has been lied to in order to bring people of color under political and economic subjection, Caucasians have also harmed themselves. They have told a lie about themselves for so long that they have become delusional by believing it. How embarrassed most of them must be, now that scientific information about the Afrikan origin of humanity and Afrika being the first and greatest cradle of civilization is everywhere, worldwide.

Common sense tells us that people who are truly superior never have to talk about it or remind others. They are too busy producing and demonstrating their intellectual and creative genius. People with superior talents and faculties are secure in their own abilities and are never threatened when others demonstrate genius or greatness.

On the other hand, it is the people who are insecure in their abilities who have a need to hold others back. This is especially true when the supposedly "superior" people have plagiarized the great accomplishments of world civilization, claiming them as their own. What a farce! What an embarrassment to learn that you owe your life's blood and the major accomplishments in your culture to the very people whom you claim are inferior. How much more ridiculous can the "superior" people look right now, in the face of so much scientific and historical evidence? In their delusional state they still attempt to deny the countless evidences of science. (Retrieved from http://realhistoryww.com/world_history/ancient/White_people.htm).

The MtDNA studies have just "put icing on the cake," so to speak, by presenting irrefutable genetic evidence about the greatness of Afrikan people. Once Afrikans around the world wake up and change themselves, they will once again take control of their national resources and adopt an ideology of cultural self-determination.

Out-of-Afrika Theory

Mitochondrial DNA genealogy research provides scientific evidence that supports the "Out of Afrika" theory. The theory claims that the entire human species is Afrikan because Afrika is where humanity first evolved, and where human beings have spent the majority of our time on Earth. Studies show that all human beings today carry DNA mutations with roots that trace back to a common ancestor who lived in Afrika some 140,000 years ago. (Retrieved from http://www.trussel.com/pre hist/news 255.htm).

DNA migration mapping shows that as ancient Afrikans spread around the world, many became isolated and developed specific mitochondrial haplogroups in the various geographic regions. As a result of their taking different migration paths, haplogroups that are specific to one group can sometimes be found in another. (Retrieved from www.kerchner.com).

According to researcher John R. Moore, "The Black Afrikan race is therefore the only original and pure race that exists today; all other so-called races are mere variations of this original Negritic race. Besides, the appearance of other races is a recent occurrence in world history, taking place after the migrations of Blacks from Afrika into Europe and Asia some 40,000 to 50,000 years ago." (Retrieved from http://webcache.googleusercontent.com/search?q=cache:http://besetfree.host56.com/chinese.html).

Genetic research has found MtDNA migration paths that agree with fossils from around 200,000 years ago. Genetic tracking of those migration paths demonstrates that all human beings trace back to a small band of females who evolved into modern human beings in Afrika. These descendents of "Afrikan Eve" migrated out of Sudan and began the grand journey into the rest of the world. These are the people who are responsible for populating and colonizing the entire Earth. Differences in physical appearance developed as climatic adaptations when modern humans left tropical Afrika and migrated into colder climates that were farther away from the equator. These scientific studies provide our best understanding of how, when, and where humanity first originated. (Retrieved from https://genographic.nationalgeographic.com/human journey/); and (http://en.wikipedia.org/wiki/Recent_Afrikan_origin_of_modern_humans).

The genetic MtDNA research findings are consistent with the "Out-of-Afrika" theory, as well as archaeological evidence that the original Homo sapiens were Afrikans who developed into modern human beings around 140,000 B.C.E. Around that time Afrikans walked out of Sudan to populate and colonize the entire world. Scientific evidence also shows that the various so-called "races" developed when Afrikans had to adapt to much colder, even arctic climates as they migrated out of tropical Afrika into the rest of the world. This process of adaptation was especially necessary for survival among those Afrikans who lived through the Ice Age in Eurasia. (Retrieved from http://humanpast.net/evolution/evolution200k.htm). Some genetic scientists believe that albinism changed from being a congenital disorder and stabilized as the norm among Europeans during the Ice Age. Albinism is characterized by a complete or partial absence of pigment in the eyes, hair, and skin. (Retrieved from http://en.wikipedia.org/ wiki/Albinism); and (http://realhistoryww.com/world_history/ancient/White_people.htm).

Mitochondrial DNA (MtDNA) is a single stranded DNA that is passed from mothers to their male and female offspring. However, MtDNA can only be passed on by females. It becomes discontinuous in males. Thus it is possible to trace the genetic lineage of any person living today back to her/his first female ancestor at the very beginning of humanity, if that female lineage remains unbroken.

Mitochondrial Eve or Genetic Eve is the name chosen by genetic scientists to refer to the original woman considered to be the mother of all human beings. She is not to be confused with the Eve mentioned in religious mythology. About 150,000 years ago she was part of a small group of females who were the "most recent common ancestors" (MRCA) of all human beings alive today. In other words, all living humans today are descendants of a few ancient Afrikan mothers. Mitochondrial Eve was not the only living female of her time. However, some of her female contemporaries failed to produce an unbroken female line that survived up until today, and others had daughters who gave birth only to sons. Both instances would break the mitochondrial line of descent because males do not pass on MtDNA. (Retrieved from http://en.wikipedia.org/wiki/Mitochondrial_Eve).

Through a genetic tracking method that goes backward in time, scientists further discovered that the numbers of those ancient mothers in Afrika diminished in an unbroken lineage with each previous generation until all those maternal lines reduced to just one female. The genetic evidence shows that 150,000 years ago her mitochondrial genes were the most successful, and the only ones to survive.

Multiregional Theory
There is a competing Multiregional theory that disagrees with the dominant Out-of-Afrika theory. Some scientists express the view that the people living today descended from several indigenous archaic human populations that

existed in the Old World, such as European Neanderthals and Peking Man in Asia. However, several different studies demonstrate without question that modern human mitochondrial DNA is of Afrikan origin. Studies conducted four years ago found that Neanderthal genes were very different from DNA of Afrikan people today.

Contrary to the Multiregional theory, there is compelling scientific support for the theory that modern humans rose out of Afrika in the past 200,000 years. In the process of leaving Afrika and venturing into the rest of the world, Afrikans eliminated populations of indigenous archaic humans like Neanderthals without interbreeding with them. NOVA conducted further DNA genetic studies and discovered that Europeans and Asians did, however, interbreed with Neanderthals. The NOVA DNA studies found around 4% Neanderthal genes in today's Caucasians and around 2% among today's Asians. (Retrieved from http://www.trussel.com/prehist/news255.htm; and
http://www.pbs.org/wgbh/nova/evolution/decoding-neanderthals.html).

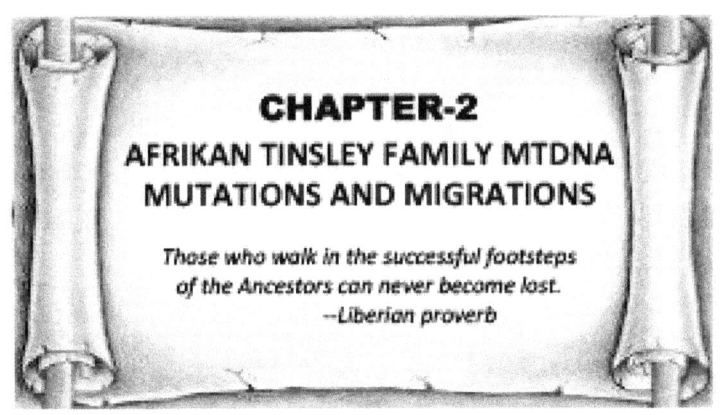

CHAPTER-2
AFRIKAN TINSLEY FAMILY MTDNA MUTATIONS AND MIGRATIONS

Those who walk in the successful footsteps of the Ancestors can never become lost.
--Liberian proverb

Genetic scientists have studied human fossils (remains) and discovered several mutations (changes) which have occurred in human haploid DNA since 200,000 B.C.E. MtDNA evidence demonstrates that the MtDNA haploid group of Afrikan Tinsleys is some of the oldest and the most varied on this Earth. Ancient Afrikan Tinsley grandmothers helped to produce a very large segment of the entire human population on this planet. This claim is supported by following the migration paths traveled by haplogroups of Tinsley prehistoric and ancient ancestors. (Retrieved from http://humanorigins.si.edu/evidence/humanfossils/species/ homo-sapiens).

The Haploid Migration Map provided by the Genebase DNA Ancestry Project shows the routes of migration taken by all Afrikan females from the beginning of modern humanity. This is how Afrikan Tinsley MtDNA has been traced all the way back in time to 200,000 years ago. (Retrieved from https://genographic.nationalgeographic.com/human-journey/).

The following information is taken directly from the Genebase Laboratory map that traces and illustrates the migration paths and MtDNA haplogroup blood mutations that occurred during Afrikan Tinsley female journeys over the course of almost 200,000 years. (Retrieved from http://www.genebase.com/ learning/ article/17).

The timeline in this document begins 200,000 years ago when Afrikans first began to migrate into other parts of the world. Scientific evidence reveals that today's various mitochondrial haploid blood types originated as MtDNA haplogroup "L" around 200,000 to 140,000 years ago. From haplogroup "L" the Afrikan Tinsley female MtDNA haploid line mutated three times, summarized as follows.

Haplogroup "L" is the most ancient of all, and is directly linked to who is referred to as

"Afrikan Eve." The majority of all Afrikans fall within Haplogroup "L." Afrikan Tinsleys in *Haplogroup "M"* populated a large portion of Asia and the Americas by mutating into haplogroups C and D. *Haplogroup "Z"* originated/mutated among Afrikan Tinsleys in Asia, and those Afrikan Tinsleys became the first settlers of Siberia. Afrikan Tinsleys next developed *Haplogroup "C"* as they continued to settle and populate much of Asia. They journeyed into Northern and Central Asia, and eventually into North America. *Haplogroup "D"* was the last mutation experienced by Afrikan Tinsleys during their journeys through Northern and Eastern Asia and the Americas. (Information taken from the *Haploid Group MtDNA Migration Map* provided by Genebase Laboratories.)

A more detailed explanation of these mutations may be helpful. Haplogroup L1, which is found primarily in West and Central Afrika, gave rise to haplogroups L2 and L3 approximately 170,000 to 150,000 years ago. DNA studies reveal that haplogroup L2, believed to have arisen around 70,000 years ago, is present in approximately one third of all people on Earth.

Haplogroup L3 is most common in East Afrika, and is found only in Afrikan populations.

However, haplogroups M and N appear to have arisen from L3, and these two are ancestral to all haplogroups outside Afrika. They represent the initial migration out of Afrika taken by modern humans. (Retrieved from http://dnahaplogroups.genebase.com/mtdnaHaplogroupSearch.php?formSubmitted=1&targetNodeId=25754194&result=haplogroup&hap=L3); and (www.kerchner.com).

Haplogroup "M" was the first Afrikan Tinsley female haplogroup mutation that occurred approximately 80,000 to 70,000 years ago. This haplogroup extends to geographic regions that include South Asia, East Asia, and Australasia. The entire indigenous population of Australia is typed as Group "M." M1 is found primarily in northern Afrika, where it appears some may have migrated back to Afrika after the first dispersal into Eurasia. Besides Asia, haplogroup "M" also populated much of the Americas about 80,000 to 70,000 years ago. (Retrieved from http://www.genebase.com/learning/article/17).

Group "CZ" expresses a combined mutation from the original "L3" haplogroup. The map shows that shortly after mutating from "L3" Afrikan Tinsleys mutated into two separate haplogroups: "C" and "Z". The Group "Z" mutation originated early on in Asia, where Afrikan Tinsley females became the first settlers of Siberia. Today Group "Z" is found in Korea, China, and Russia. Group "C" Afrikan Tinsley females journeyed further into Siberia, Northern and Central Asia, and eventually into North America. (Retrieved from http://www.genebase.com/learning/article /17).

Group "D" arose about 60,000 years ago when Afrikan Tinsley females traveled into Asia. This haploid blood group is found today in northern and eastern Asia and in the Americas. Afrikan Tinsley Haplogroup "D" is one of the oldest mutations in the world, and is the most extensive, followed closely by Group "C". (Retrieved from http://www.genebase.com/learning/ article/17).

The following Migration Map (**Figure-3**) illustrates the journeys of all haplogroups over a period of some 200,000 years. The locator for the origin of "Afrikan Eve" is "**L3.**"

FIGURE-3

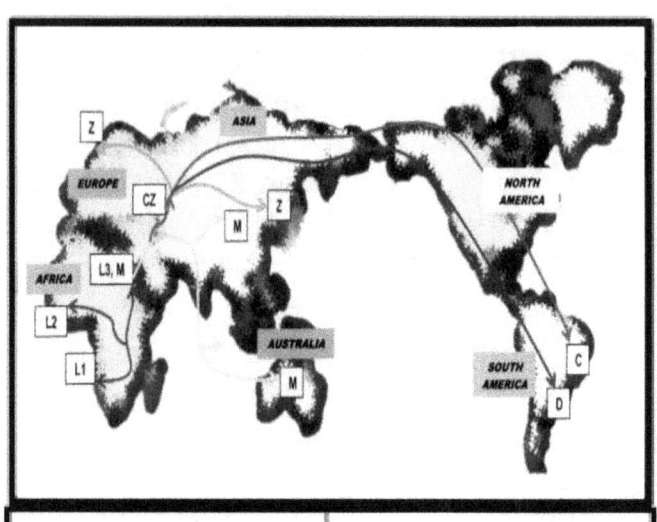

L1 : 200,000 BCE	M : 80,000 BCE
L2 : 170,000 BCE	CZ: 70,000 BCE
L3 : 150,000 BCE	D : 60,000 BCE

This ancient Afrikan Tinsley family study is in agreement with scientific MtDNA regression studies which show the genetic relationship of all human beings going as far back as 230,000 B.C.E. The studies are based upon the "Out-of-Afrika" Theory which states that humanity began in Afrika, and that Afrikans are the oldest expression of humanity. The haploid studies gathered genetic samples from women all over the world to form their data base. Their scientific findings corroborate the findings of noted historians and archaeologists: that Afrikan people populated the entire Earth; and that they originated every civilization in the world.

The following chapter coordinates the data provided by Genebase Laboratories on Afrikan Tinsley bloodline migration routes with documented archaeological evidence of prehistoric human development. The book itself attempts to present information in layman's terms that includes prehistory, archaeology, and genetics.

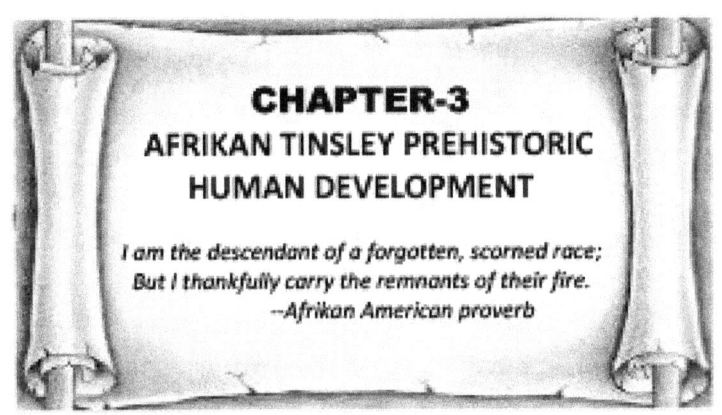

CHAPTER-3
AFRIKAN TINSLEY PREHISTORIC HUMAN DEVELOPMENT

I am the descendant of a forgotten, scorned race;
But I thankfully carry the remnants of their fire.
--Afrikan American proverb

Early Human Development

The evolution of modern humans and the factors that triggered their development are some of the most important events in human prehistory. Most scientists agree that the human species is an Afrikan species. Fossil evidence demonstrates that all humanity originated in Afrika and evolved to the level of modern humans (Homo sapiens) between 200,000 and 140,000 B.C.E. during a time of dramatic climate change. Earth's climate suddenly cooled, introducing the onset of the Ice Age. Afrikan Tinsley ancestors at that time gathered and hunted food and developed cultural behaviors that supported survival. (Retrieved from https://genographic.nationalgeographic.com /human- journey/).

There is controversy as to how and why early humans became omnivores, eating fruits, plants and animals. Some scientists claim that the change from herbivore to omnivore occurred early on in human development. It was certainly an evolutionary advantage for our ancient ancestors to be able to eat just about anything and everything. One strong argument claims that becoming meat eaters is how humans rose to the top of the food chain. Contrary to "meatarian" views that humans are "natural" carnivores, humans lack the physical and biochemical equipment of natural carnivores and omnivores. Humans never developed the natural abilities necessary to outrun wild animals; catch hold of them with sharp talons; tear apart their flesh with specialized teeth; eat raw flesh without chewing it; and properly digest raw animal flesh. (Retrieved from http://www.ecologos.org /omni.htm; and http://www.npr.org/blogs/thesalt/2012/04/20/150817741/for-most-of-human-history-being-anomni vore-was-no-dilemma).

It was the development of human culture that allowed humans to expand their diet to include the eating of animal flesh. The development of group hunting, the creation of sharp killing and cutting tools, the later invention of the throwing spear, and the use of fire to cook raw meat and fish are some of the necessary cultural developments that allowed early humans to become successful carnivores. Once ancient ancestors began to domesticate fruits, plants, and animals, the human diet consistently became omnivorous, which included meat (Retrieved from http://www.vrg.org/nutshell/omni.htm); and http://www.npr.org/blogs/thesalt/2012/04/20/150817741/for-most-of-human-history-being-anomnivore-was-no-dilemma).

Out of Afrika

As modern humans our ancient Tinsley ancestors were among the modern humans that migrated out of the Afrikan homeland and eventually colonized the entire Earth. They became sole survivors in the human family tree. By modern humans we mean *Homo sapiens* of 200,000 to 140,000 years ago who shared important characteristics with humans today. Their anatomical features (skull shape and size) and behavioral attributes (use of blades, bone tools, pigments, burial goods, art, trade, hunting, and varied environmental resources) were not significantly different from today's humans.

During the Ice Age modern human explorers were newcomers to Eurasia, which was the ancestral home and natural environment of Neanderthals. Modern humans and Neanderthals existed together in Eurasia for perhaps 15,000 years. Generally speaking, modern humans were physically very different from Neanderthals. Their brains were about the same size, but their skulls were shaped differently. Modern humans were a slimmer, taller, more smooth-skinned, less hairy breed. Their facial anatomy was also different. Modern humans had high, rounded foreheads with a more pronounced nasion depression at the root of the nose just underneath the eyebrows. The modern newcomers' skulls were flatter in back than the Neanderthals', and they had prominent jaws. Their rounded foreheads did not have the heavier Neanderthal brow ridges.

In scientific terms modern humans had a "gracile" physique: smaller in stature than Neanderthals, with more pronounced sexual dimorphism (differences). Neanderthals, on the other hand, had a "robust" physique; heavy-boned, very hairy, with flat, sloping foreheads and heavy brow ridges. Modern humans' molars gradually reduced in size and their teeth developed thicker enamel as they increasingly became omnivores. Their lighter bodies may have meant that they needed less food, giving them a competitive advantage during hard times. (Retrieved from http://web.missouri.edu/~flinnm/courses/mah/factfiles/australopithecus.htm).

Modern humans' cultural behaviors were also different. Neanderthals made tools, but they worked with chunky flakes struck from large stones. Modern humans' stone tools and weapons usually featured elongated, standardized, finely crafted blades. Both species hunted and killed the same large mammals, including deer, horses, bison and wild cattle. However, moderns' sophisticated weaponry made them more successful, i.e.: a variety of throwing spears made from carefully wrought stone, bone and antler tips. In addition, modern humans' tools may have kept them relatively safer. Fossil evidence shows Neanderthals suffered grievous injuries such as gorings and bone breaks, probably from hunting at close quarters with short, stone-tipped pikes and stabbing spears. Modern humans' throwing spears probably required fewer close-quarter encounters. (Retrieved from http://human

origins.si.edu/evidence/human-fossils/species/homo-sapiens).

Both species had rituals. Both buried their dead, and both made ornaments and jewelry. Some researchers believe the Neanderthals were learning these behaviors from the moderns. Modern humans produced their artifacts with a frequency and expertise that Neanderthals never matched. As far as researchers know, Neanderthals had nothing like the etchings, bone carvings, and ivory flutes found at Blombos Cave in South Afrika. The mesmerizing cave paintings and rock art that modern humans left in Blombos Cave are like snapshots of their world. (Retrieved from http://popular-archaeology.com/issue/September-2011/article/100-000-year-old-art-work shop-discovered-in-south-africa).

After migrating out of Afrika into Eurasia, Afrikan Tinsleys subsequently spread into Micronesia, Polynesia, and the "New World" comprising what is now known as North and South America, Latin America, and the Caribbean. They probably didn't migrate with any specific destination in mind. Instead, they most likely traveled into territories that were favorable for their survival. Many Afrikan Tinsley ancestors probably chose coastal routes where both fish and game were plentiful. (Retrieved from (http://humanorigins.si.edu/evidence/human-fossils/species/homo-sapiens).

Migration, Colonization, and Early Civilizations

Genetic DNA studies suggest that around 140,000 years ago ancient Afrikan Tinsley ancestors began migrating out of Afrika by various routes. They traveled from Sudan through the Middle East and across the Straits of Gibralter, eventually populating and colonizing the Earth. By 130,000 B.C.E. they began to exchange resources with other explorers over long distances. (Retrieved 10/25/13 from http://www.telusplanet.net/dgarneau/ euro2.htm).

Between 90,000 B.C.E. modern Afrikan Tinsleys began to make special tools for fishing. Archaeologists found artifacts in Cape Town, South Afrika which reveal that by 80,000 B.C.E. early human technology had advanced to where they also produced spearheads. According to the archaeologists, this craft took a long time to learn. Early humans had to acquire a lot of knowledge for spearhead production.

Producing stone spearheads for throwing spears also required the ability to plan in several stages. That complicated crafting process affected the development of the human brain and its ability to think and reason. Tool-making also developed the working memory and social life of early humans. Knowledge of the technology was passed from one generation to the next, from adults to children. It became part of a cultural learning process which created a more advanced society than before. In addition, the technology led to increased social interaction both within and across the generations. This happened because the crafting of stone spearheads took a long time to learn and required a lot of theoretical and practical knowledge. This social learning process contributed to the subsequent development of early modern humans' cognitive (mental and intellectual) ability to express symbolism and abstract thoughts through their material culture. As a result, they began to create artwork in the form of decorated objects. (Retrieved from http://hnn.us/article /140276).

According to the genetic and paleontological records, between 80,000 and 60,000 B.C.E. modern Afrikan Tinsley ancient ancestors continued to migrate out of Afrika and populate the world. From about 80,000 B.C.E., Arctic ice spread south until it covered vast regions of northern Europe, Asia and America under glaciers hundreds of feet thick. In some places the ice is thought to have been two miles thick. The only relief for the people during those times was that the winters did not become more bitter. Summers, on the other hand, became much colder, giving the winter ice no chance to melt. The following winter's ice added to that of the previous year and never thawed. For thousands of years the ice grew into a huge wall beyond which people could not venture. (Retrieved from (https://genographic.nationalgeographic.com/human-journey/).

About 74,000 B.C.E. modern humans almost became extinct as a result of extreme climate changes. The population may have been reduced to about 10,000 adults of reproductive age. However, Afrikan Tinsley females were among the few who survived to carry humanity on into the future. (Retrieved from http://www.telusplanet.net/dgarnea/ euro2.htm).

Into Australia, Asia, and Polynesia

Recent genetic studies published in 2009 by the Genome Organization Pan-Asian Consortium have discovered that Asia was originally settled by Afrikans who migrated into what is now India. From there they continued on into southeast Asia and the islands of the Pacific. They later journeyed up to the eastern and northern mainland of Asia. These early Afrikans migrated into and settled in the new location. They established new civilizations in each of these places. (Retrieved from http://en.wikipedia.org/wiki/Sun daland).

__Australian Aboriginal Civilization__

Afrikan Tinsley ancestors migrated east into Australia and China around 70,000 years ago. Some members of the group "island hopped" across the Indian Ocean to northern Australia and Papua New Guinea, where both are part of the same land mass. It appears that they then moved farther inland by following the Australian river systems.

Two mysteries surround this voyage which represents one of humanity's first great achievements. The first mystery is concerned with why a small faction of Afrikan Tinsley ancestors decided to break off from the main group to make the voyage from Asia into Australia. The second mystery involves the kind of water vessels capable of making such a voyage 70,000 years ago. Some scientists suggest that primitive boats or rafts made from bamboo were used, since bamboo is a common material in Asia. These adventurous Afrikan Tinsleys literally discovered a new, unpopulated continent and claimed it for their own. In Australia Afrikan Tinsley ancestors began the Aborigine civilization. Present-day Australian Aboriginal people are the oldest population of humans living outside of continental Afrika. (Retrieved from https://geno graphic.National geographic.com/migration-to-aus tralia/).

According to findings of genetic migration mapping and DNA recombination studies, some Afrikan Tinsleys stayed behind in each new land they explored and made it their home. Journeying through Asia, they established the Indus Valley civilization. In China they created the Xia and Shang civilizations, which were the very first civilizations in that country. Over time, in Burma and Thailand they created the Ban Chiang and Mon civilizations. Traveling further into Asia, they created the Khmer kingdoms of Funan and Angkor. In Vietnam, they created the Champa civilization, and in Japan they started the Momon and Ainu cultures. (Retrieved from http://real history.ww.com/world_history/ancient/cro_magnon_Homo_sapien.htm).

Linguists have discovered that the original languages of South China, Taiwan, and Vietnam were all originally Afrikan languages. Researchers have actually gathered documentation and recordings from Afrikans that detail their journies to and from the Melanesian Islands, South China, and the Americas. They report traveling as early as 3,000 B.C.E. from East Afrika and from across the Sahara before it became a desert. Retrieved from http://community.webtv.net/nubianem.

Indus Valley (Harappan) Civilization

DNA research findings show that Afrikan Tinsley ancestors settled in southern Asia about 70,000 B.C.E. Archaeological evidence reveals that the straight-haired Dravidian Afrikans who did not have "Mongol" features took a coastal route across what is today southern Arabia and traveled along the coast of southern Asia. There is some controversy as to whether the first group of Dravidians traveled into southern Asia around 70,000 B.C.E. or if they migrated there 60,000 years ago. Whichever is the case, they made a second wave of migration around 50,000 B.C.E. This latter group was probably led by the big game hunters who crossed Southern Arabia, but followed an inland route in search of game. The Dravidians stayed close to Afrika and settled in the region of Southern Asia that is now called India. (Retrieved from http://www.mapsofindia.com/myindia/history/facts-about-the-indus-valley-ivilization).

In India the Dravidian Afrikan Tinsleys created the Harappan or Indus Valley Civilization, which is one of the earliest urban civilizations in the world. Around 5,000 years ago they built brick cities and public works with irrigation; had a roadside drainage system; and constructed an efficient plumbing system. Their cities were laid out in residential blocks with multi-storied brick houses. Scholars have noted an enduring Afrikan influence in Harappan Civilization. Close similarities still exist between the Indus Valley Civilization and the Nile Valley Civilization of ancient Egypt. This is not strange, because: (a) the Dravidians migrated out of northeast Afrika; and (b) geographically, the ancient Indus Valley

Civilization extended all the way to Egypt for a very long time.

Evidence shows that Afrikan Tinsley ancestors created a notably peaceful society in the Indus Valley. Researchers have found no weapons, which signifies that there was no war or conflict in Harappan Civilization. It also appears that all Indus Valley citizens enjoyed equal status, with no sign of rulers. (Retrieved from http://indusvalley.edublogs.org/what-is-so-special-bout-the-indus-valley/).

There is linguistic evidence of the ancient Afrikan origins in the Indus Valley in the form of Cushitic languages. Researchers have discovered that the people of South India are of direct Afrikan origins. Research findings reveal that the Sudras, the Panchamas, and many other groups ranging from Sri-Lanka to Bangladesh are of ancient Afrikan origins. The languages of these groups are related to Eastern Afrikan languages. (Retrieved from http://dalitstan.org/books/sudroidhttp://dalitstan.org/sudroid/books).

Chinese Civilization

The Genebase migration map shows that the main contingent of Afrikan Tinsley ancestors continued their trek through Asia. They reached what is now China around 60,000 B.C.E. where they created the Xia and Shang civilizations, the very first civilizations in China's history. (Retrieved from http://realhistoryww.com/worldhistory/ancient/China2.htm).

The fact that China has several pyramids is still a well-kept secret. Tinsley ancestors were most likely carriers of this architectural knowledge. Chinese archeologists discovered these structures some time ago, but the information has not been made available to the general public or the world. This is perhaps due to China's political situation. It is well known that pyramid building originated in Afrika. Therefore, it can be strongly suggested that this knowledge was carried into China at some later time. (Retrieved from http://realhistoryww.com/world_history/ancient/China_1.htmhttp://realhistoryww.com/world_history/ancient/Olmec_the_Americas.htmTheOlmec and the Americas).

Many physical features that have been evident among Afrikan people from Sudan, Congo, and South Afrika for more than one million years are clearly similar to those among East Asian and East Indian people. Some of those features include: small to tall stature, kinky hair, black to brown skins, high cheekbones, and slanted eyes with a fold of skin on the upper eyelid that partially covers the inner corner of the eyes. (Retrieved from http://www.asiafinest.com/forum/index.php?showtopic=40115).

Afrikan Tinsleys developed the first recorded history in China, beginning with the Shang Dynasty. They also developed the Yangshao culture, which is dated up to about 3,500 B.C.E. and is directly related to the Xia Dynasty. Yangshao culture created the first evidence of advanced farming and surplus food production in China. They cultivated millet, rice, and soybeans. They also domesticated pigs, cattle, sheep, dogs, chickens, and possibly the horse as well as silkworms. We know that ancient Afrikan Tinsley females invented agriculture around 10,000 B.C.E., so it is not difficult to claim their participation in developing the Yangshao culture and the Xia Dynasty civilization. Researchers found elaborately worked artifacts made of jade, flint, bone, and stone. (Retrieved from www.ushistory.org/civ/9b.asp).

Genebase Laboratory data concerning Afrikan Tinsleys are in agreement with the research findings of Chinese Professor Jin Li of the Fudan University of Shanghai. Additionally, Li's international team of researchers discovered evidence that is in agreement with the Out-of-Afrika "Single Origin" theory. This aspect of the Out-of-Afrika theory argues that Afrikans are the ancestors of all humanity. Li's international research team in Shanghai was comprised of scientists from Russia, India, Brazil, and other nations. Their five-year research project found that the early human ancestors of Chinese people originated from East Afrika and migrated into China along South and Southeast routes in Asia. This is the very route that Genebase Laboratory data reports as being the one taken by Afrikan Tinsley women. Li's team of scientists further argues conclusively that their DNA studies demonstrate an Afrikan origin of Chinese people; findings which the researchers say correspond with the fact that "all 65 branches of the Chinese race share similar DNA mutations with the peoples of East and Southeast Asia." (Retrieved from http://www.trinicenter.com/FirstChinese.htm).

Professor Li's research team findings nullify the theory that the Chinese race evolved from Peking Man, who lived in northern China 400,000 years ago. The Chinese team based their findings on the DNA analyses of about 100,000 samples gathered from around the world, along with the geographic and genealogical routes related to the spread and settlement of modern humans. The following link contains information for direct contact with Dr. Jin Li in Shanghai. (Retrieved from http://www.trinicenter.com/FirstChinese.htm).

Further evidence of Afrikan Tinsley presence in Chinese early civilization comes from the Chinese people themselves. They perform a semi-annual Chinese ritual that takes place on the 10th full moon of the lunar calendar deep in the mountains of Miaoli and Hsinchu. The event is called the "Ritual of the Little Black People," and it has been performed by the Saisiyat tribe for the past 100 years. According to the Saisiyat people, the ritual keeps alive the spirit of a race of Afrikan people who are said to have preceded all others in

Taiwan. Another huge festival in commemoration of the Little Black People is held every 10 years. During the ritual and the festival, Saisiyat people are not supposed to fight or engage in any type of disturbance. Taiwanese people also refer to them as the "Little Black People." Chinese historians call these diminutive, dark-skinned people with the broad noses and curly hair "Black Dwarfs," and recognize them as the most ancient human beings on Earth. These references to the Little Black People are directly related to ancient Tinsleys. (Retrieved from http://www. trinicenter .com /FirstChinese .htm).

According to eyewitness reports as well as scientific studies, the kin of these Africoid people continue to survive throughout Asia today in the Phillipines, northern Malaysia, Thailand, Sumatra, Indonesia, and other places. People of the Saisiyat tribe say the "Little Black People" gave them seeds and taught them to farm. So we see again the Afrikan Tinsley females carrying their knowledge of agriculture into areas of the world outside the Afrikan continent. (Retrieved from http://www.taipeitimes.com/News/feat/archives/2004/11/27/2003212815);

(http://www.telusplanetnet/dgarneau/euro2.htm; and
(http://realhistoryww.com/worldhistory/ancient/China_2.htm).

Linguistic studies lend even further support to an Afrikan origin of Chinese civilization. There are thousands of names commonly found from Sudan to Senegal and from the Sahara to South Afrika that are identical in sound to both Chinese and Japanese. Some of those names which are still used today include Kong, Cheng-Cheng, Ming, Yang, Anyang, Kwango, Chu, Wong, Fang, Ddong, Deng, Ndongo, and others. Based upon Genebase data, Tinsley journeys and explorations are responsible for the spread of these names. (Retrieved from http://www.asiafinest.com/forum/index.php?showtopic=40115).

Philippines

Afrikan Tinsleys left further indelible historical marks in Asia as they settled in the Philippines and created new civilizations. Some Chinese scholars claim that the languages and people of the Philippines have Afrikan origins, and that these Africoid peoples actually brought their culture into Southeast Asia. Many of these original

Afrikans came into the Philippines by way of india, which accounts for the term "Indo-China." (Retrieved from http://www.asiafinest.com/forum/index.php?showtopic=40115).

Researchers at the Max Planck Institute for Evolutionary Anthropology in Leipzig, Germany have study findings which demonstrate Afrikan Tinsley presence in ancient Asia. They discovered that a small Philippine tribe known as the Mamanwa have Afrikan origins. The original Mamanwa are said to be a small band of Afrikans that broke away from their original group in the process of migrating out of Afrika some 36,000 years ago. In their DNA study the researchers found a common genetic origin for Australian, New Guinean, and Philippine Mamanwan peoples. These are the geographic regions in which Genebase Laboratory data show people have only Tinsley haplogroup "M" MtDNA. (Retrieved from http://www.sciencedaily.com/releases/2013/01/130114152952.htm).

This migration into the region of the Philippines occurred long before the Sahul land mass broke up into islands about 8,000 years ago. The Sahul was once a sizable land mass above sea

level, but warped downward and subsided as a result of rising sea waters. It is suggested that Afrikan Tinsleys migrated out of Afrika using the Sahul land mass in their continued trek across Asia into what is now known as the Philippines. The submerged Sahul Shelf is presently a stable structural shelf or platform on the Pacific Ocean floor. It extends from the northern coast of Australia to the island of New Guinea. (Retrieved from http://digitaljournal .com/article/ 341937); and
(http://www.britannica.com/EBchecked/topic/516502/Sahul-Shelf).

Researchers from Leeds University in West Yorkshire, England conducted a MtDNA study which made similar findings. Their 2009 study, conducted under the auspices of the Human Genome Organization Pan-Asian SNP Consortium, also concluded that Asia was originally settled by modern humans who migrated from Afrika into India. This Afrikan migrating group continued into Southeast Asia and on into what are now the Pacific Islands, and then later up to the eastern and northern Asian mainland. All the above studies validate and corroborate Genebase Laboratory data concerning the migration patterns of Afrikan Tinsley females. (Retrieved from http://en.wiki pedia.org/wiki /Sundaland).

Japanese Civilization

About 35,000 to 30,000 years ago a group of Afrikan Tinsley ancestors continued to journey across Asia, eventually migrating into eastern and southeastern Asia. Some of them settled in the region that is now the Japanese Islands. In Japan they created the Jomon and Ainu cultures. The Jomon were the first humans to inhabit the Japanese Islands. Their semi-sedentary culture consisted of hunting, gathering, fishing, and tool-making. The group known as the Ainu followed later. Africoid human fossils have been found throughout all the Japanese islands. Today, Afrikan genes are still present in 40% of modern Asians, including the Japanese, Mongolians, and Tibetans. (Retrieved from http://realhistory ww.com/world_history/ancient/Misc/Japan/The_Jomon.htm); and (http://realhistoryww.com/world_history/ancient/China_2.htm).

Malaysian Civilization

In Indonesia, the Afrikan Tinsleys created the Orang Asli culture of Kuala Lampur in Malaysia. Nicholas Wade (2005) bases his

research on recent MtDNA studies reported by Dr. Vincent Macaulay of the University of Glasgow, along with his team of genetic scientists who traced Orang Asli MtDNA from Afrika. The research team found evidence which shows that a single band of modern hunter-gatherer Afrikans migrated into the region that is now called Malaysia by taking a southern route to India, Southeast Asia, and Australia. (Retrieved from http://www.nytimes.com/2005/05/13/science/13migrate.html?_r=0); and
(http://realhistoryww.com/world_history/ancient/cro_magnon_Homo_sapien.htm).

Burma and Thailand Civilizations

Afrikan Tinsleys eventually created the Ban Chiang and Mon civilizations in what is now the region of Burma. Although humans lived in Burma as early as 11,000 years ago, archaelogical evidence shows that the first settlements began around 2500 B.C.E. with cattle raising and bronze production. The Mon people first settled in the Ayewarwaddy River region. Afrikan Tinsley females' haploid MtDNA was also traced to the Ban Chiang people of Northeastern Thailand from around 11,000 to 10,000 B.C.E. Further indication of Tinsley female cultural influence is that they left evidence of permanent villages where the people grew rice, domesticated water buffalo, and produced bronze and iron technology. (Retrieved from http://realhistoryww.com/world_history/ancient/cro_magnon_Homo_sapien.htm); and (http://en.wikipedia.org/wiki/Migrationperiodofancient Burma).

Polynesian Islands

According to the Genebase laboratory report, Afrikan Tinsleys settled the Polynesian Islands. As verification, scientists have found that people in the Pacific Islands originally came from Southeast Asia. We have already discussed the dispersal of modern man out of Afrika, and how part of this migration reached Southeast Asia by 60,000 B.C.E. This group then continued to migrate from Southeast Asia into the Pacific through the regions now called New Guinea to Australia and the Bismarck Archipelago about 45,000 years ago. (Retrieved from http://lens.auckland.ac.nz/images/3/31/Pacific_Migration_Seminar_Paper.pdf).

Ancient Tinsley female movement into new areas stopped for almost 30,000 years, until a later wave of expansion occurred into the rest of the Pacific around 3,500 B.C.E. This later expansion journeyed east to Samoa and Tonga and from there north to Hawaii. Their expansion also went further east to what is now Easter Island and south into today's New Zealand. According to genetic researchers, this was the last major human migration event. (Retrieved from (http://realhistoryww.com/world_history/ancient/Misc/Americas/Australians_and_Polyn.htm); and (http://www.ncbi.nlm.nih.gov/pmc/articles/PMC1801234/).

Scientists Adele Whyte and Geoff Chambers bring new insight to the above information. By comparing the DNA of people from Asia, across the Pacific Ocean, and on to New Zealand, these two researchers found that Maori men and women arrived from different homelands. A migrating group of around 56 women hopped from island to island. They started with Taiwan and arrived in New Zealand 800 to 1,000 years ago. Apparently, Afrikan Tinsley women were in this group. The researchers also found that as the Maori women and men migrated from island to island, Melanesian men joined the boats. This resulted in the diversity of today's Maori population. These research findings are strengthened by the fact that archaeological evidence and Maori legends are in agreement with the research claims. (Retrieved from http://www.abc.net.au/science/articles/2003/03/27/817069.htm); and (http://lens.auckland.ac.nz/images/3/31/Pacific_Migration_Seminar_Paper.pdf).

The Americas and the Caribbean

Ancient Afrikan Tinsley females did not stop with the settling of several regions in Asia. The people who became their Asian descendants made their way into the Americas and the Caribbean between 40,000 and 15,000 B.C.E. With each new land into which they journeyed, some Afrikan Tinsleys continued the tradition of staying behind to make it their home. Thus, people of the Afrikan Tinsley MtDNA haplogroup became founders of more civilizations in the Western hemisphere.

Three Afro-Asian groups left Asia and migrated into the Americas by travelling from Siberia and Beringia. These two regions are close to the Bering Strait, the Bering Sea, and the Chukchi Sea. They crossed over by using what is called the Bering Land Bridge that connected Asia and North America during the Pleistocene Ice Age.

This land bridge melted when the climate became warmer around 11,700 years ago. (Retrieved from http:// phys.org/news/2013-09-mitochondrial-genome-north-american-migration.html).

The first Afro-Asian females of Tinsley lineage that migrated into North America is the most ancient of those found in the Americas. They populated the Americas from Canada to the southern tip of Chile. MtDNA analyses reveal that while most of the Native American populations arose from the first Tinsley Afro-Asian migration, two subsequent migrations occurred. The second and third migrations resulted in an Arctic population and civilization who today speak Eskimo-Aleut languages, and the Canadian Chipewyan civilizations who speak the Na-Dene language.

In the new lands of North America Tinsley Afro-Asians developed a Native American civilization similar to the Old World civilization which they left behind. Tinsley knowledge of agriculture, astronomy, mathematics, architecture, creative arts, religion, writing, and other skills emerged among the people as they began to create the new Native American culture.

Presently, the genetic makeup of the first migratory group makes up 50% of contemporary Eskimo-Aleut speakers' DNA, and 90% of the Chipewyans' DNA. The two later groups merged with the first group after they arrived in the Americas. The DNA of these two later groups is more closely related to present-day Asian populations. This is because many Eskimo-Aleut speakers migrated back into Asia over time, carrying what had become Native American genes back into Asia resulted in a genetic re-mixture. (Retrieved from http://phys.org/news/2013-09-mitochondrial-ge nome-north americanmigration .html).

Afrikan Tinsley women have been discussed above from the beginning of humanity and traced throughout the world as they journeyed across the Earth exploring, settling, colonizing, populating, and creating world civilizations. The number of individual researchers and research teams that have independently reached the same conclusive findings must be taken into consideration where questions of validity are concerned. This study mentions only a handful of them. Many other studies exist besides these that are in agreement with both the Genebase Laboratory data and the Out-of-Afrika theory.

What follows is further information pertaining to ancient Tinsley cultural accomplishments along the way.

CHAPTER-4
AFRIKAN TINSLEY CULTURAL ACCOMPLISHMENTS

Until the Lion begins to tell his own story,
The tale of the hunt will always be given
From the perspective of the hunter.
--Kenyan proverb

It is not possible to discuss how human culture developed without taking Afrika as a starting point. Afrika is the very origin and cradle of human civilization. Those carrying the Afrikan Tinsley female haploid bloodline were there from the very beginning, along with some other bloodlines.

Use of Fire

Scientists believe that the control of fire was very likely a key factor in the migration of Modern Afrikans Tinsleys' migration out of Afrika into Eurasia more than a million years ago. The discovery and control of fire provided warmth, light, and protection from animal predators. More importantly, fire gave them the confidence to leave their circumscribed surroundings to venture forth into new, unfamiliar environments. Thus, had it not been for their knowledge of how to control fire, Afrikan Tinsleys and other haploid groups might never have left the Afrikan homeland. (Retrieved from http://www.sciencedaily.com/releases/2008/10/081027082314.htm).

Along with the control of fire came the practice of cooking food began some 1.8 million years ago. Tinsley ancestors discovered that cooking meat made it easier to chew and digest. It also killed off bacteria that existed in the meat. Scientists believe that the meat protein helped the human brain to develop into its present form. Early ancestors also learned that more energy is gained from cooked food—energy that was critically needed for survival in extremely strenuous circumstances. Cooking also made certain roots and grains edible and easier to chew. (Retieved from http://news.discovery.com/human/evolution/cooking-meats-ancestors.htm).

Over time ancient Afrikan Tinsley Grandmothers elevated the practice of cooking food to an art form. Their culinary skills have been passed down through the ages, and supported Afrikan survival during slavery. For thousands of years Afrikan traditional culture has associated Afrikan women with three critical functions: (a) the mastery and control of fire; (b) the art of cooked food; and (c) the beginning and support of civilization through agricultural development. Throughout Afrika today women continue to control farming and markets, which gives them a huge participation in their nations' economies.

Women in Culture, Art Creation, and Religion

Archaeologists note a burst of culture among Afrikan Tinsleys and other haploid groups of modern humans between 60,000 and 40,000 B.C.E. Scientists refer to this sudden burst of culture as the "Upper Paleolithic Explosion." Sudden major progress appeared in tools, personal adornment, habitations, burials, art, language, and social organization. The men began to create more sophisticated spear tips and cutting/chopping implements. Women began to create jewelry and to use bones to make sewing needles and fishing hooks. Afrikan Tinsley women and men began to weave nets for fishing and hunting. (Retrieved from http://books.google.com/books).

Afrikan Tinsleys created permanent drawings, an indication that they were capable of abstract thought. Scientists note several important physiological developments that accompanied the creative and technical innovations that occurred during 60,000 and 40,000 B.C.E. Abstract artistic images from that period are evidence that modern humans had begun to develop important cognitive abilities. Scientists point out that art is evidence of the beginning of symbolic thought, reasoning, and mental activity found in modern humans today. The art of that period is also seen as being evidence of religious thinking and shamanism, although some believe religion may have first emerged as far back as 200,000 years ago. Ancient Tinsley women were a part of this artistic legacy from long ago. (Retrieved from http://www.sciencedaily.com/releases/2008/10/081027082314.htm).

Afrikan Tinsleys were among the first humans to develop both female and male shamans. Shamanism might have been a more or less natural occurrence once a sense of spirituality and God-consciousness began emerged among human beings. Those who demonstrated superior spiritual gifts such as clairvoyance, healing, prophecy, etc. were most likely selected to be spiritual leaders. Religious beliefs and practices became culturally embedded among groups. These modern humans began to conduct rituals when they buried their dead. Flowers, colored stones, arrow tips, and other items were found in the graves. (Retrieved from http://books.google.com/books).

Denita Benyshek, Ph.D. (2012) has conducted years of extensive research on ancient female artists and shamans. She reports that some Western male researchers have wrongly referred to cave artists as being exclusively male. She reports that for almost 100 years male chauvinist researchers have knowingly imposed their "androcentric bias" by using masculine pronouns and by making specific comments to that effect, as well. She reveals that these biased researchers have intentionally ignored the valid research findings which clearly show that women played important leadership roles in both the spiritual and cultural lives of their communities. (Retrieved from https://www.academia.edu/2066714/Artists_as_Shamans_Historical_Review_and_Recent_Theoretical_Model).

Benyshek (2012) cites some of the accurate studies which show evidence that early female shamans are the ones who actually created a lot of the drawings, engravings, and sculptures found in caves. Benyshek's (2012) citations reveal that her claims are corroborated by noted archaeologists who have published their findings in prominent scientific journals for years. It is almost certain that Tinsley women were among these early female shamans. (Retrieved from https://saybrook.academia.edu/DenitaBenyshekPhDMFA);
and (https://saybrook.academia.edu/DenitaBenyshekPhDMFA).

Strengthened Social Relationships

Cultural traditions, rituals, and social differentiation arose along with human language around 50,000 B.C.E. Strengthened social relationships as well as kinship bonds and trade with other groups occurred between 60,000 and 40,000 B.C.E., along with population increase and the propensity to colonize. Given the important roles that women have always played in family and society, it is certain that Afrikan Tinsley females were instrumental in strengthening social relationships in the ancient past. (Retrieved from http://www.evfit.com/40,000 ya. htm#symbolic).

Invention of Agriculture

A major turning point occurred in human development and civilization between 11,000 and 10,000 B.C.E. when Afrikan Tinsley females invented agriculture. The practice of agriculture further strengthened intragroup and intergroup social relationships. Our ancient grandmothers discovered they could control the growth and breeding of certain wild plants and animals. This domestication of plants and animals led to farming and herding. The activities of those ancient women laid the foundation for world civilization because settlements, villages, towns, and cities cannot exist without the support of farms. As farms grew, human populations also increased dramatically because stored food made feeding larger numbers of people for longer periods of time possible. In turn, more people meant even greater agricultural development. In this manner Afrikan Tinsley women helped to transform Earth's natural landscapes locally at first, then globally.

About 9,000 B.C.E. Afrikan Tinsley ancestors continued to lay the foundation for world civilization as they cultivated increasingly large farms. Agriculture became more and more intensive. Sedentary, permanent lifestyles began to replace nomadic hunting and gathering ways of life. The revolution in food production created the world's first population explosion. Having a reliable food supply led to the first early cities about 8,000 B.C.E. Cities developed complex societies, and these developed into modern civilizations. Metal-working, writing, and other technological inventions were improving many lives by 7,000 B.C.E.

First Math Calculator
Around 10,000 and 22,000 B.C.E., Afrikan Tinsley ancestors witnessed the invention and use of the world's first math calculator. Use of this device was very useful in intergroup trade relations, and supported further agricultural development. Markings on the bone indicate that it was used as a counting tool for conducting simple mathematical procedures. It is named the "Ishango Bone" because in 1960 it was discovered in the area of Ishango, centered near the

headwaters of the Nile River at Lake Edward. Ishango lies on the border between modern-day Uganda and Kongo. Afrikan Tinsleys definitely used this counting device to conduct trade, given that Angola lies within the same general region as Ishango. (Retrieved from: http://en.wikipedia.org/wiki/ Ishango_bone).

Scientists first believed the artifact to have been created about 10,000 B.C.E. However, further tests reveal that it was created more than 20,000 years ago. This has created some controversy in the scientific community because writing, calculation, and mathematics often develop simultaneously. Therefore, it can be speculated that West Afrikans in Uganda and Kongo may have had writing as well as mathematics long before Afrikans in Sumer and Egypt around 4,000 B.C.E.

Invention of Steel

Most of the world doesn't realize that it was East Afrikans who first invented steel independently around 2,000 B.C.E. The Genebase MtDNA migration map places Tinsley females there at the time among the Bahaya or Haya people in northwestern Tanzania. They were the first to learn how to produce high carbon steel. American archaeologist and historian Peter R. Schmidt (1997)[5] actually witnessed a re-enactment, by Bahaya elders, of the traditional iron smelting process as it has been performed for thousands of years. (Retrieved from http://gakondomedia.wordpress.com/2012/11/26/invention-of-steel-in-the-kingdom-of-karagwe/).

It was made clear to Schmidt (1997) that the knowledge and techniques of iron production have not been lost. The Bahaya elders demonstrated how indigenous natural resources and local invention were used in the process. They used the formula Fe_3O_4 to produce steel. They added this to the top of the furnace with charcoal as the source of carbon. The air entered the furnace through a greatly enlarged system of air bellows at the bottom. This preheated the air to around 1800 degrees Centigrade—a temperature much hotter than was ever reached before with conventional-sized bellows. Steel invention revolutionized weapons production and made iron ore and bronze weapons outmoded. Europe never

---

[5] Schmidt published his findings in a 1997 book entitled: "Iron Technology in East Africa: Symbolism, Science, and Archaeology." Bloomington, Indiana: Indiana University Press.

had a high quality of steel comparable to East Afrikan steel until around 1800 C.E. (Retrieved from http://gakondomedia.wordpress.com/2012/11/26/invention-of-steel-in-the-kingdom-of-karagwe/).

Steel is actually an alloy of iron, and Schmidt (1997) found proofs that iron technology has a long history in Afrika before the invention of steel. Chemistry and metallurgy analyses of the East Afrikan smelting process have been conducted that validate the ancient indigenous nature of East African iron. Schmidt (1997) found similar reports of iron inventions and workings around the Great Lakes Region of East Africa. Physical evidence was discovered in excavations, in rock paintings, and in iron-related tales among the Cwezi, Tutsi, Nyambo, Baganda, Luo, and Kikuyu people. (Retrieved from http://gakondomedia.wordpress.com/2012/11/26/invention-of-steel-in-the-kingdom-of-karagwe/).

Metal Cutting Tools

Metal cutting tools were used to cut down trees, and from this practice wood carpentry began. The use of metal tools rapidly expanded farming by making the clearing of trees and land cultivation much easier. Thus iron, the development of metallurgy, and the creation of metal implements created a second wave of revolutionary cultural changes in the world; changes that included the use of metal weapons for warfare. (Retrieved from http://human past.net/evolution/evolution200k .htm).

First Writing Systems

Modern linguistic scholars have grouped the 5000 or so world languages into less than 20 categories, based upon the shared words, sounds, or grammatical constructions that link them to each other. These scholars hold the theory that each linguistic group descended from one common ancient ancestor, and that ancestral language was of Afrikan origin. Therefore, this method of grouping languages agrees with the Out-of-Afrika theory. Afrikan Tinsley female ancestors were among those who developed the first writing systems. It is important to understand that a shared linguistic family does not mean that a racial link exists between languages. (Retrieved from http://www.history world.net/wrldhis/plaintexthistories.asp?history id=ab13#ixzz302ygqwob).

Sumer and Egypt

In Sumeria Afrikan Tinsleys were among the first Afrikans to invent writing in the region of Mesopotamia around 4500, B.C.E. Writing was created in Egypt around the same time. The first form of writing was the pictorial stage. Separate symbols were created for writing and numbers, so writing and mathematics developed together. The writing system began with cumbersome pictograms and hieroglyphics.

As civilization became more complex, an increasingly complex and abstract form of writing was required. Cuneiform writing came to represent both sounds and meanings for objects, and concepts. Cuneiform writing originated as a system of pictorial drawings. Thus, over time the number of pictographs became smaller as they became more abstract. The original Sumerian script was the basis of Akkadian, Eblaite, Elamite, Hittite, Luwian, Hattic, Hurrian, and Urartian languages and script. (Retrieved from http://www.historyworld.net/wrldhis/PlainText Histories.asp?historyid=ab33); (http://www.historiasiglo20.org/egypt/mesopotamia.htm); and (http://en.wikipedia.org/wiki/Sumerian_script).

Second Writing System: Indus Valley

Indus script, developed around 2500 B.C.E. by Indus Valley civilization, is also referred to as Harappan script. To date, Indus script has not been deciphered, although scholars have attempted to do so for almost 70 years. Several theories exist, but the most promising one to many scholars points to its being of Dravidian origin. Arguments in favor a Dravidian origin of Indus Valley writing makes sense when placed within the context of the Out-of-Afrika theory. This implies that Afrikan Tinsley females were among carriers of other ancient haploid MtDNA haploid lines who migrated out of Sudan into Asia and developed this writing system there. (Retrieved from http://www.ancientscripts.com/indus.html).

Third Writing System: China

Linguists believe that the first system of writing in China originated around 1600 B.C.E. during the Shang Dynasty. Most of archaic Chinese writing survived on bones, bronze, and turtle shells. Writings from the ancient Shang Dynasty are the direct ancestor of modern Chinese characters. Chinese characters are broadly used throughout Asia in countries such as Japan, Korea, and Vietnam. Afrikan Tinsley ancestors who settled in some of these Asian countries were probably instrumental in helping to develop the Chinese, Japanese, Korean, and Vietnamese writing systems. (Retrieved fromhttp://en.wiki pedia.org/wiki/History_of_writing#Chinese _writing).

Fourth Writing System: Mesoamerica

Writing did not reach the Americas until about C.E. 600. The oldest known scripts in the Americas are those of the Olmec peoples of Mexico. The Olmecs were the first major civilization to establish themselves in Mexico, where they settled in the south-central tropical lowlands. Their ancestral lands were in the modern-day states of Veracruz and Tabasco. They were the first Mesoamerican or Middle-American civilization to develop. As such, the Olmec peoples laid many important foundations for other Mesoamerican civilizations and societies that followed. (Retrieved from http://en.wikipedia .org/wiki/Mesoamerican_writing_systems).

The laboratory test has demonstrated that Afrikan Tinsley blood was carried as far as the Native Americans in the western hemisphere.

Some researchers believe that the ancient Olmecs were related to the people of Afrika. They base their claim on the facial features and Afrikan-styled corn-row braids of several colossal Olmec statues, pyramids, as well as countless Olmec artifacts. According to Afrika-centered scholars, the combined evidence clearly shows that Afrikans were present in Mesoamerica around 800 to 700 B.C.E. Scholars such as Leo Wiener, Ivan Van Sertima, Clyde Ahmad Winters, and others identify the Olmecs with the Mande people of West Afrika. Some scholars have demonstrated that some Olmec symbols are similar to those in the Vai script. The Vai language is part of the larger family of Mande speakers in West Afrika. These claims are not widely accepted by many researchers. (Retrieved from http://en.wikipedia.org/wiki/Indigenouslanguages_of_the_Americas).

This is the extent to which this book goes in tracing the voluntary migrations of Afrikan Tinsley women for a period of some 140,000 years. The next chapter examines the tribal information provided by the Genebase Laboratory. According to Genebase mtDNA findings, the Mbundu Tribe of Anola, West-Central Afrika is our tribe of origin.

Tinsleys have the same MtDNA haploid type as the Mbundu people today.

The next chapter briefly discusses the history of the Mbundu people of Angola who proudly claim the great warrior Queen Nzinga as one of their former monarchs.

CHAPTER-5
AFRIKAN TINSLEYS: FROM ANGOLA TO VIRGINIA

To get lost is to learn the way.
-- Afrikan proverb

Angola and Kongo C.E. 1200 to 1600

Genebase laboratory findings reveal that Afrikan Tinsleys share the same haploid group with people in the Mbundu/Ambundu Tribe who were brought into the western hemisphere from Angola between 1600 and 1800 C.E. The genetic test also reveals a tiny fraction of a haploid line found in people from neighboring Kongo. Therefore, the historical relationship between precolonial Angola and Kongo have to be presented here.

Between precolonial periods 1200 and 1500 C.E. Mbundus/Ambundus, a Bantu people, migrated into the Angola region from North Afrika, bringing agriculture with them. Being farmers, they built permanent settlements and villages. The region of precolonial Angola held a rich diversity of several distinct ethnic communities: the Ambundu; the Ovimbundu; the Bakongo; the Chokwe; and some others.

Afrikan Tinsley females were in this group of Mbundu/Ambundu who spoke the Kimbundu language. Their society was both matriarchal and matrilocal. Grandmother's MtDNA reveals that her haploid blood type is found today primarily among the Mbundu/Ambundu people of Angola; but her blood also has traces of a haploid blood type shared by people in the Kongo.

Today the Kongo shares the same border with Angola on the coast of West Afrika, and their joint history is directly connected with Grandmother's MtDNA. The first King of Kongo occupied part of Mbundu territories and turned MPemba into his province in 1370. Not stopping there, the Kongo Kingdom also laid claims to Matamba, Ndongo, and Kisama Kingdoms by 1480. This political affiliation makes it highly probable that marriages took place among people from both Mbundu and Kongo Kingdoms. (Retrieved from en.wikipedia.org/wiki/Culture_of_Angola).

The King of Kongo had a monopoly on trade with the Portuguese in the 15th century. When a NDongo leader tried to break this monopoly in 1482, it led to a war after which NDongo Kingdom won its independence. Once freed from Kongo domination, the NDongo Kingdom allied itself with the nearby Matamba Kingdom in the 16th century, around 1590. The alliance of people in these two kingdoms gave them the courage to directly confront Portuguese colonialism and the capturing of slaves. This alliance bravely engaged in ongoing warfare against the Portuguese for 14 years. However, their defeat in 1614 made the people in both of these Afrikan kingdoms targets for the slave trade. Huge numbers of the Mbundus, who also carried small amounts of Kongo people's MtDNA blood type, fled to neighboring states. However, some Afrikan Tinsley females were captured and brought into the western hemisphere. (Retrieved from http://en.wikipedia.org/wiki/Ambundu).

It is proposed that this is the manner in which Tinsley females were among the very first Afrikans to be brought into the Virginia colony from the Angola/Kongo Kingdoms of West-Central Afrika from 1619 onwards. They were part of the large slave system established by the Portuguese to supply slaves to the Spanish colonies in Central and South America. (Retrieved from http://en.wikipedia.org/wiki/Culture_of_Angola).

From Angola to the Virginia Colony

The State of Virginia was originally founded as an English colony in 1618 by the London Virginia Company. In 1624 the Virginia Company was dissolved by King George III and Virginia became a royal colony controlled directly by the British government. The first Afrikans taken into Virginia included Tinsley women from the Angola/Kongo regions of West-Central Afrika in 1619.

The Portuguese originally supplied slaves to Spanish colonies in Central and South America. However, two English pirate ships operating in the Caribbean raided a Portuguese ship in the Gulf of Mexico and transported them to Jamestown, Virginia instead. The ship that transported them was called the "White Lion." Most Afrikans brought into Virginia were imported from Barbados in the Caribbean islands. Rarely were they shipped to the American colonies directly from Afrika. Jamestown and Yorktown were the two locations in Virginia where most of the Afrikans landed. It is unknown as to whether the status of the early Afrikan Tinsleys in Virginia was as servants or slaves. What is known is that Afrikans were put to work as laborers on tobacco plantations alongside English indentured servants. (Retrieved from http://www.encyclopediavirginia.org/Colonial_Virginia).

Virginia established the headright system in order to solve both its population and its labor shortages. This system involved a legal grant of land to settlers from Europe, and was principally responsible for the expansion of the 13 British colonies. Anyone willing to cross the Atlantic Ocean and help populate the American colonies was granted from 1 to 1,000 acres of land. Landowning masters could then pay for the transportation costs of a laborer or indentured servant. Indentured servants remained poor because they had little or no chance to procure their own land. (Retrieved from http://historyisfun.org/pdf/From-Afrika-toVirginia/TheAngolanConnection.pdf).

In November 1609 Powhatan Indians laid siege to Jamestown, which denied White colonists access to food sources. Tremendous suffering resulted, called the "Starving Time." By Spring 75 percent of Whites in Jamestown were dead from hunger and disease. This war lasted until 1614. A labor shortage developed after a second Anglo-Powhatan war broke out in 1622, which caused English servants to be reluctant about agreeing to immigrate into Virginia.

With the high demand for laborers to maintain the plantation agriculture, the economic solution was to bring in laborers from Afrika through the Caribbean islands as well as directly from the continent. By the 1650s Virginia planters increasingly had to rely on people from Afrika to work the labor-intensive tobacco plantations. Tinsleys were among these workers. There was no organized, systematic trade in slaves between Afrika and Virginia in the middle of the century. Slave ships made unplanned, irregular stops in Virginia in the process of trading in the Caribbean or Central Afrika. (Retrieved from http://en.wikipedia.org/wiki/History_of_slavery_in_Virginia); and
(http://www.encyclopediavirginia.org/Colonial_Virginia).

At first there was a very small population of Afrikans in Virginia. They worked alongside White servants in the tobacco fields, and often even lived with them. However, as Afrikan populations increased, plantation owners began to create separate quarters for Afrikans and Whites. Slave quarters ranged from one individual or family group to more than a dozen unrelated strangers from different cultures, often speaking different languages. As a rule, slave owners did not respect marriage or kinship ties, and families were often not allowed to live together in the same quarter. (Retrieved from http://en.wikipedia.org /wiki/History_of_slavery_in_Virginia).

The slave system in Virginia developed over a period of time. It was not inevitable at first that all Afrikans who arrived there from 1619 on were made slaves. By the middle of the century almost a third of all Afrikans in Virginia colony were free persons. Some had arrived as free persons or had been born to free parents. Most had been either slaves or indentured servants at some time. Free Afrikans had similar lifestyles as their English neighbors, although most were poorer than other free persons. They held property, paid taxes, married, and raised their families just like Whites.

In some cases they prospered enough to acquire plantations of their own. Free Afrikans had surnames that were usually adopted from former White masters. They interacted with Whites, Native Americans, as well as with enslaved and other free Afrikans. Up until the 1670s free Afrikans even had the legal right to own slaves and White indentured servants. The slaves they owned were most often family members, parents, children, spouses, and lovers who were purchased from White plantation owners in order to free them. In return, those family members gladly worked and generally helped out in various ways to repay the financial sacrifice that paid for their freedom. (Retrieved from http://en.wikipedia.org/wiki/History_of_slavery_in_Virginia).

In 1710 most Afrikan slaves had been born in Afrika. This changed, however, as more women were included. There was an increase in the number of slaves born in Virginia because of the women giving childbirth. Around 91 percent of Afrikans were born in Virginia by 1770, and many were sired by White plantation owners. Over time a distinct culture developed among Afrikans that was different from Anglo/English culture. Their storytelling, music, and dance were distinctively different. They developed a Creole language (Ebonics) which linguistic researchers have discovered still uses the English lexicon/words, but linguistically fits squarely within the Niger-Kordofanian family of West Afrikan languages. (Retrieved from http://www.encyclopediavirginia.org/Colonial_Virginia).

As the century progressed the rights and status of free Afrikans were reduced. Every year between 1667 and 1672 the Virginia General Assembly established the legal framework for perpetual slavery based on skin color. Virginia began to revise its laws, making Afrikan slavery a permanent status generation after generation. Similar laws followed in 1680, 1682, and 1686. As slaves Afrikan Tinsleys no longer worked by mutual agreement, nor for a limited period of time. Permanent slavery became a necessary economic factor for the labor-intensive tobacco plantations of Virginia. By 1705 slavery was established at every level of society in Virginia. In 1723 a law was passed that restricted "Negros,

Mulattos, and Indians, bond or free" from voting. The law even restricted White masters from freeing their slaves. (Retrieved from http://www.encyclopediavirginia.org/Colonial_Virginia).

Despite the laws that attempted to control them, Afrikans in Virginia rebelled often. Many of them simply ran away. Others planned open insurrection. Some were part of the "Servants' Rebellion" of 1663. In 1687 several Afrikan slaves conspired to kill Whites and destroy their property. The next stage in the development of slavery was motivated by a sharp reduction in the value of sugar grown in the Caribbean. As a result, plantation owners there began to sell their Afrikan slaves to the tobacco farmers in Virginia. By the final decade of the 17th century, around the 1690s, the legal foundation was solidly laid for an 18th century plantation society. There is a continuing debate as to which came first in Virginia: racism against Afrikans; or a legal system that supported the economics of the plantation system. (Retrieved from http://en.wikipedia.org/wiki/Jamestown,Virginia); and (http://www.encyclopediavirginia.org/Colonial_Virginia).

The situation in the Caribbean boosted the tobacco economy of Virginia for a while. Tobacco had been the staple crop in Virginia since the early 1600s, and for a while economic benefits gained from growing tobacco were great. However, this situation took a downward turn over time for several reasons. The availability of fertile land dwindled. Over-worked soils on the old plantations became exhausted. These problems were accompanied by a sharp decrease in demand for tobacco. These developments resulted in diminished economic opportunities for the average tobacco grower in Virginia. Some free Afrikans were forced onto marginal lands, and others left Virginia altogether and migrated to northern colonies. Some Afrikan Tinsleys may have been among those free women and men migrating out of Virginia (Retrieved from http://mshistory.k12.ms.us/articles/169/the-great-migra tion-to-the-mississippi-erritory-1798-1819).

From Virginia to Mississippi and Other States

Up to this point, the Genebase Laboratory report was used to trace Tinsley genetic lineage from 140,000 B.C.E. to 1600 C.E. In their efforts to help in the research effort for this book, some Tinsley family members were scrambling to find the connection between the family line from Virginia to other states. This changed dramatically when extensive genealogical records of the Caucasian Tinsleys were discovered online just days before the deadline for submitting the book for publication. Those records show how Afrikan slaves on the Tinsley plantation(s) were forcibly taken from Virginia farther into the Deep South during the late 1700s and early 1800s.

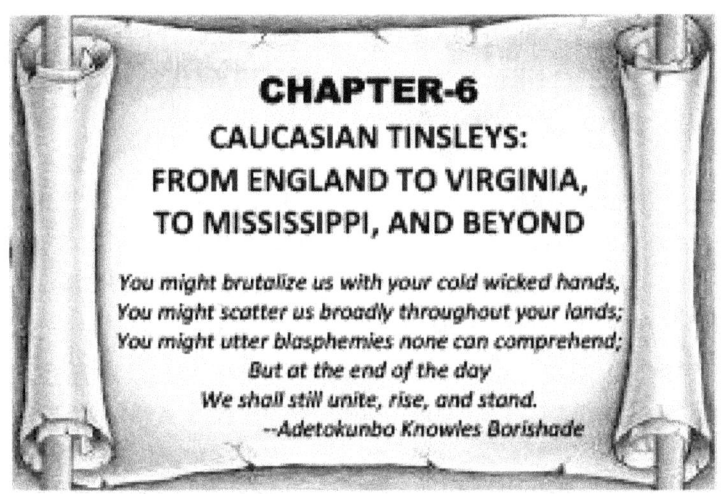

CHAPTER-6
CAUCASIAN TINSLEYS: FROM ENGLAND TO VIRGINIA, TO MISSISSIPPI, AND BEYOND

You might brutalize us with your cold wicked hands,
You might scatter us broadly throughout your lands;
You might utter blasphemies none can comprehend;
But at the end of the day
We shall still unite, rise, and stand.
--Adetokunbo Knowles Borishade

Caucasian Tinsley Family

Migration Into Mississippi

Thomas Tinsley emigrated from Yorkshire, England and arrived in the British colony of Virginia in 1638. His transportation was paid by John Robins of James City County, Virginia. Before he came to purchase any land of his own, Tinsley lived by a creek known as Moses Run. His fortunes increased over the years, such that December 13, 1650 he was able to purchase 300 acres in the Moses Run area. He bought another 300 acres in 1662 on the south side of York River in New Kent County, Virginia. By then he was well on his way to becoming a wealthy plantation owner with slaves of his own. That is where the ancestors from Angola took on the Tinsley name. (Retrieved from http://www.kemper.msgen.info/firstfamiles/tinsley_family_history.htm.

Caucasian Thomas Tinsley married Elizabeth Randolph and shortly after built his home near Totopotomoy Creek located 12 miles north of what is now Richmond, Virginia. Court records note that she may have been born in England prior to her marriage, or perhaps she met Thomas in New Kent County, Virginia after he immigrated there. The date of their marriage was 1638, the same year of Thomas Tinsley's arrival. Therefore, the couple most likely met in Virginia because English custom would not have allowed a single woman to travel far away from home on a man's promise to marry later. Thomas and Elizabeth had several children: Thomas Tinsley II; John Tinsley; Cornelius Tinsley; Betty Tinsley; Agnes Tinsley; Alice Tinsley; and Rachel Tinsley. As adults they, in turn, established their own plantations with slaves that carried the Tinsley name. Some Afrikan Tinsleys may even have been sired by White Tinsley planters. (Retrieved from http://www.kemper.Msgen.info/firstfamilestinsley_family_history.htm.)

Thomas Tinsley became a very prosperous business man. He not only exported his tobacco from Virginia to England, but also imported domestic luxuries and clothing. Throughout Virginia his successful business ventures caused him to be considered a man of great influence, esteem, and courage. He is reported to have lived in both New Kent and Hanover Counties. Early documents list his last name with various spellings: Tilsley (1638); Tilsey (1650); and Tinslie (1655). According to records, it is uncertain as to whether Thomas Tinsley died in New Kent or Hanover County in 1702. His wife Elizabeth survived him. In accordance with English custom, Thomas Tinsley's will left the bulk of his estate to his eldest son Thomas II. (Retrieved from http://www.kemper.msgen.info/firstfamiles/tinsley_family_history.htm.); and (http://freepages.genealogy.rootsweb.ancestry.com/~mysouthernfamily/myff/d0000/g0000068.html#I39294).

Many of the Caucasian Tinsleys remained in Virginia after the death of their father Thomas. However, some of the successive generations joined other White plantation owners who carried some 500,000 Afrikan slaves with them as they migrated out of Virginia into new territories like Mississippi, Alabama, Georgia, Louisiana, Florida, and Missouri. Congress organized the Mississippi Territory in 1798 and opened it for White pioneer settlement. White planters swarmed out of Virginia believing they could improve their fortunes in these new fertile lands that lay further West. Westward migration by White farmers became so great during the first 20 years of the 19th century that historians refer to it as the "Great Migration." This is not to be confused with the "Great Migration" of Afrikans out of the Deep South into northern states after Reconstruction in 1867. (Retrieved from http://mshistory.k12.ms.us/articles/169/the-great-migration-to-the-mississippi-territory-798-1819).

Outstanding economic opportunities were promised to White Virginia planters who were willing to venture westward into the Deep South. In the 1790s, the prospects for supplying the foreign demand for southern cotton were met by the invention of the cotton gin. By 1800 Kentucky and Tennessee were the only two territories established as states west of the Appalachian Mountains. By 1820 there were eight, including Kentucky, Tennessee, Ohio, Louisiana, Illinois,

Indiana, Mississippi, and Alabama. The State of Mississippi—which is Grandmother Elizabeth Tinsley's home—was apparently caught up in this massive migration. Her grandparents and others were forcibly carried from Virginia into Mississippi territory by White slave masters.

Kemper County, Mississippi was formed in 1833. However, Caucasian planter John Tinsley—probably the great-grandson of Thomas Tinsley--was a resident in the area since 1817. He is listed in the state Census and the land tax rolls from 1837 through 1850. It is noted in Census records that he had three Black male slaves at that time: John Tinsley; James B. Tinsley; and Thomas Tinsley. White planters John Henry Tinsley, Green Tinsley, and others left Georgia to settle in Kemper County, Mississippi. (Retrieved from http://www.kemper.msgen.info/firstfamiles/tinsley_family_history.htm.

The *Kemper County, Mississippi 1850 Slave Schedule* compiled by Marleen Sue Van Horne (1999) lists more than 1,200 African Americans in Kemper County alone. Of that number, three free Black male Tinsleys are listed: James B. Tinsley; John Tinsley; and Thomas Tinsley. One Black male slave, also named John Tinsley (age unknown), was included in this list. This information is corroborated by Kemper County Census data of 1850 which reports that all three were, indeed, residents in 1850, and it is clear they were owned by or worked for the White planter John Tinsley. (Retrieved from http:// www.kemper.msgen.info/census/1850_Slaves/1850-alpha.txt).

The 1870 Census of Kemper County lists White planter John Tinsley's son (age 30) and his two daughters Hattie/Harriett (age 22) and Mattie (12). Several more slaves or Black workers were added to the Caucasian Tinsley family roles: William Tinsley, mulatto; Sell Tinsley, black; Allen Tinsley, mulatto; and Ned Tinsley, black. By that time several more White Tinsleys had moved into the County, having migrated in from Georgia, Alabama, and South Carolina. (Retrieved from http://us-census.org/pub/usgenweb/census/ms/kemper/1850/sl00027.txt).

Even more White Tinsleys moved into Misissippi. Caucasians Elizabeth Tinsley and John Tinsley were residents in Monroe County, Mississippi. It appears that they owned one female slave, also named Elizabeth Tinsley. The

1870 Census of Warren County show yet another Caucasian John Tinsley who was married to Matilda Robinson on the role. Afrikan Isaac Tinsley, also of Warren County, may have been closely associated with them. In 1900 an Afrikan woman Susan Tinsley appeared in the Warren County Census. In 1870 a marriage certificate was issued to Afrikan Arthur Tinsley and his bride Frances McNeil in Copiah County. (Retrieved from http://us-census.org/pub/usgenweb/census/ms/kemper/1850/sl00027.txt).

There is much more research to be conducted in seeking out Grandmother Tinsley's roots. However, more cannot be done at this time. At least this chapter satisfies the question as to how and why Afrikan Tinsleys got from Virginia to Mississippi and other states in the Deep South.

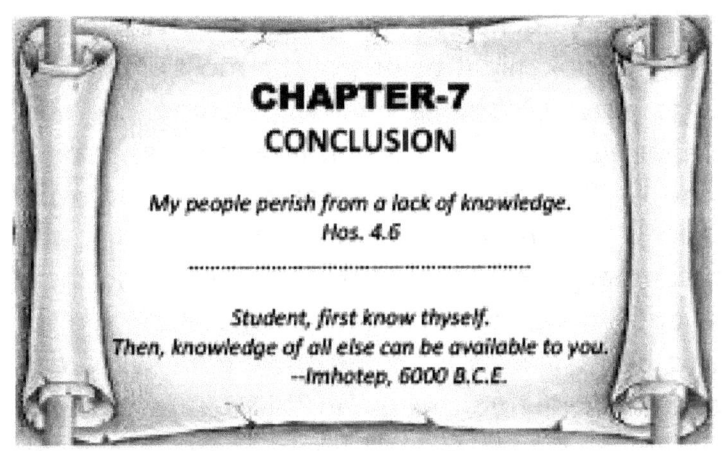

CHAPTER-7
CONCLUSION

My people perish from a lack of knowledge.
Hos. 4.6

Student, first know thyself.
Then, knowledge of all else can be available to you.
--Imhotep, 6000 B.C.E.

Knowledge of oneself, one's family legacy, and one's culture is one of the most empowering elements that a human can possess. **History** is a timeline that lets you know about the people who contributed to your spiritual makeup, your psychological wellbeing, and your physical environment from the time you were born. It informs you of survival lessons learned through trial and error. It teaches you whom to trust and distrust. **Culture**, on the other hand, provides the self-affirming, pro-social ideals, beliefs, values, and total way of life that ensure survival, independence, and autonomy.

Once I began this project it occurred to me that this book might be one of the most important things I have accomplished in my lifetime. There is a lingering feeling that this publication may inspire some life-changing future events. Therefore, this book is submitted as an inspiration for my contemporaries to do as I have done. I hope they will add their ancient ancestors' legacy to mine so as to begin filling in the historical gaps with real personal family narratives. In this manner I hope this book stands as a documented historical contribution to future generations.

Imagine what would happen if Afrikans representing all 21 haplogroups were to conduct similar studies, then began to hold ongoing seminars and international conferences in order to combine them. Such research documents would literally begin to span the whole of Afrikan contributions to humanity and civilization across the entire Earth from the beginning of time as we know it. A sharply-defined image of just who Afrikan people are would emerge for the world to see. The onus is on us, not others. We should not expect our slave masters to liberate us.

To my family I say: "those to whom much has been given, much is expected in return." The historical narratives presented within this book should be read to your children and grandchildren into perpetuity. Exchange some of the fairy tales with these narratives so that the young ones know from their most tender years that it is their legacy. Let them know that our people walked this Earth for tens of thousands of years when there was no one else besides them. Let them know that our people created the first and the highest civilizations in the world. Let the children know that they can create even greater things in their lifetimes.

If you teach your children well at home from the time they are born, by the time they get to pre-school and kindergarten no one will be able to convince them they are inferior or that our people never did anything noteworthy. Those children will be walking, talking, **nobles** with the fire of Afrikan consciousness in their brains and bellies. They will know that ancient history and world history are Afrikan history. They will understand that world religions are re-interpretations of Afrikan religion. They will be grounded in the fact that world civilizations, cultures, and traditions were founded by Afrikan ancestors. Knowledge of these things and more will be rooted in their hearts; watered by the streams, rivers, and oceans of scientific evidence; and empowered with life by God.

   I close this book knowing that it is only the beginning of something which I have no power to foresee at this time. I now delegate to the Tinsley family and to my Afrikan World family the responsibility of extending this family-based legacy from the point where I have left off. GOD BLESS YOU ALL.

REFERENCE

Sertima, Ivan Van (1976). *They Came Before Columbus: Afrikan Presence in AncientAmerica.* New York: Random House.

ONLINE TOPICAL REFERENCE SOURCES

Genetic MtDNA Studies

1. http://www.genebase.com/learning/article/17
2. https://genographic.nationalgeographic.com/human-journey/
3. http://dna.ancestry.com/
4. http://ghr.nlm.nih.gov/handbook/basics/dna
5. http://www.dnaancestryproject.com/index.php?gclid=CJHn19zBxLoCFRFo7AodByUA_g&l=n&__atoken=__NONE__
6. http://www.mcdonald.cam.ac.uk/genetics/labpubs.htm

The Beginning of Humanity

1. en.wikipedia.org/wiki/Timeline_of_human_prehistory.
2. http://www.telusplanet.net/dgarneau/euro2.htm
3. http://archaeology.about.com/od/temporalstudies/u/human_history.htm

4. http://thewordofme.wordpress.com/human-prehistoric-timeline/
5. http://web.missouri.edu/~flinnm/courses/mah/factfiles/australopithecus.htm
6. https://genographic.nationalgeographic.com/human-journey/
7. http://humanorigins.si.edu/evidence/humanfossils/ species/homo-sapiens.
8. http://humanpast.net/evolution/evolution200k.htm).
9. http://en.wikipedia.org/wiki/Recent_Afrikan_originof_modern_humans.

Human Evolution
1. http://humanorigins.si.edu/evidence/human-fossils/ species/homo-sapiens
2. http://web.missouri.edu/~flinnm/courses/mah/factfiles/australopithecus.htm
3. http://humanorigins.si.edu/human-characteristics/change
4. http://www.historyofinformation.com/
5. http://humanhistorytimeline.com/
6. http://en.wikipedia.org/wiki/Recent_Afrikan_origin_ofmodern_humans

Humans Develop as Omnivores
1. http://www.ecologos.org/omni.htm

2. http://www.npr.org/blogs/thesalt/2012/04/20/150817741/for-most-of-human-history-being-an-omnivore-was-no-dilemma
3. http://www.vrg.org/nutshell/omni.htm
4. http://www.npr.org/blogs/thesalt/2012/04/20/150817741/for-most-of-human-history-being-an-omnivore-was-no-dilemma
5. http://humanorigins.si.edu/evidence/human-fossils/ species/homo-sapiens
6. http://www.bbc.co.uk/news/science-environment-15565654

Afrcan Migrations: Population & Colonization of the Earth

1. http://www.genebase.com/ learning/ article/17).
2. http://www.trussel.com/prehist/news255.htm
3. http://humanorigins.si.edu/human-characteristics/change
4. http://www.sciencedaily.com/releases/2007/05/070509161829.htm
5. http://www.ask.com/question/what-is-the-out-of-Afrika-theory
6. http://news.nationalgeographic.com/news/2008/02/080221-human-genetics.html
7. https://www.google.com/search?q=ancient+Afrikan+migration&tbm=isch&tbo=u&source=univ&sa=X&ei=RNRlUsD0F-m-

QWqpoGwBg&sqi=2&ved=0CEgQsAQ&biw=1280&bih= 709
8. http://www.telegraph.co.uk/science/9489047/Skull-shows-early-mans-migration-to-Asia.html.
9. http://webcache.googleusercontent.com/search?q=cache:http://besetfree.host56.com/chinese.html.
10. http://realhistoryww.com/world_history/ancient/cro_magnon_.

Dravidian Afrikans
1. http://arutkural.tripod.com/tolcampus/drav-Afrikan.htm
2. http://www.beforebc.de/all_Afrika/AreDravidiansAfrikanOrigin.pdf
3. http://bafsudralam.blogspot.com/2010/09/dravidians-and-aryans.html
4. http://Afrikancivilizations.wordpress.com/2012/03/24/dravidians-of-south-india-are-an-Afrikan-people/
5. http://www.telusplanet.net/dgarneau/euro2.htm
6. http://www.mapsofindia.com/my-india/history/facts-about-the-indus-valley-civilization

7. http://indusvalley.edublogs.org/what-is-so-special-about-the-indus-valley/

Afrikans Began Ancient Canaan and Phoenician Civilizations
1. http://realhistoryww.com/

Afrikans Began Ancient Elam and Persian Civilizations
1. http://realhistoryww.com/

Afrikans Founded Ancient Indus Valley Civilizarions
1. http://realhistoryww.com/

Afrikans Began Australian Aboriginal Civilization
1. http://www.cosmosmagazine.com/news/dna-confirms-aboriginal-australian-origins/
2. http://www.bbc.co.uk/news/science-environment-15020799
3. http://www.raceandhistory.com/Science/AboriginesOrigin2.htm

Afrikans Began Chinese Civilizations
1. http://webcache.googleusercontent.com/search?q=cache:http://besetfree.host56.com/chinese.html

2. http://realhistoryww.com/world_history/ancient/China_2.htm
3. http://www.telusplanet.net/dgarneau/euro2.htm
4. http://www.trinicenter.com/FirstChinese.htm
5. http://www.taipeitimes.com/News/feat/archives/2004/11/27/2003212815
6. http://www.asiafinest.com/forum/index.php?showtopic=40115
7. http://personal.uncc.edu/jmarks/pubs/Enc%20race%20Sci%20Racism%20Hist.pdf
8. http://www.everyculture.com/South-Asia/Sudra.html
9. http://realhistoryww.com/world_history/ancient/China_1.htmhttp://realhistoryww.com/world_history/ancient/Olmec_the_Americas.htmThe Olmec and the Americas

Afrikans Began Japanese Civilizations
1. http://clockofdestiny.com/om.htm
2. http://www.stewartsynopsis.com/Stanton%20Files/black_race.htm
3. http://realhistoryww.com/world_history/ancient/Misc/Japan/The_Jomon.htm

Afrikans Began Cambodian Civilizations
1. http://www.youtube.com/watch?v=jKUEs9tV9NO
2. http://www.cambodianallianceforthearts.com/cambodia-civilization-and-historical-Afrikan-influence/
3. http://www.Afrikaresource.com/rasta/sesostris-the-great-the-egyptian-hercules/the-khmer-hindus-of-cambodia-black-asian-history-by-oguejiofo-annu/
4. http://realhistoryww.com/world_history/ancient/The_Mon_Thailand.htm

Afrikans Began Thailand Civilizations
1. http://realhistoryww.com/world_history/ancient/The_Mon_Thaland.htm

Afrikans Began Philippine Civilizations
1. http://www.asiafinest.com/forum/lofiversion/idex.php/t40115.html
2. http://digitaljournal.com/article/341937

Afrikans Began Malaysian Civilization
1. Associated Press, 2005

Afrikans Began Polynesian Civilizations
1. http://www.abc.net.au/science/articles/2003/03/27/817069.htm
2. http://lens.auckland.ac.nz/images/3/31/Pacific_Migration_Seminar_Paper.pdf

Afrikans Began Taiwan, Vietnam Civilizations
1. http://community.webtv.net/nubianem

Sumerians, Akkadians, Assyrians, Babylonians Were Afrikans
1. http://realhistoryww.com/
2. http://bafsudralam.blogspot.com/2010/12/sumerians-and-akkadians-were-blacks.html
3. http://bafsudralam.blogspot.com/2010/03/sumerians-and-akkadians.html
4. http://www.reddit.com/r/AskHistorians/comments/14lunp/are_the_sumerian_and_akkadian_related_or_totally/
5. http://lc5827wdp.com/2013/09/13/sumer-akkad-black-kushites-of-sumer-0-akkadian-later-assyrians-empire/
6. http://www.youtube.com/watch?v=Mcj9HB2-SBQ
7. http://www.youtube.com/watch?v=cSTspZkA2fw

8. http://realhistoryww.com/world_history/ancient/sumer_Iraq_4a.htm

Invention and Global Development of Writing
1. http://en.wikipedia.org/wiki/History_of_writing
2. http://www.wwnorton.com/college/english/worldlit2e/short/ch/01/timelines.aspx
3. http://edsitement.neh.gov/lesson-plan/cuneiform-writing-system-ancient-mesopotamia-emergence-and-evolution
4. http://www.historyworld.net/wrldhis/PlainTextHistories.asp?historyid=ab33

The Americas and the Caribbean
1. http://www.des.ucdavis.edu/faculty/Richerson/Speed.htm.
2. http://phys.org/news/2013-09-mitochondrial-genome-north-american-migration.html.
3. http://www.ncbi.nlm.nih.gov/pmc/articles/PMC 1801234/

Mexico's Collossal Head Sculptures
1. http://en.wikipedia.org/wiki/Olmec_alternative origin_speculations

2. https://www.google.com/search?q=olmec+colossal+heads+Afrika&tbm=isch&tbo=u&source=univ&

sa=X&ei=oahtUrn5EoH82wXbuYBY&ved=0CEAQsAQ&biw=1061&bih=542

Ishango Bone
1. http://en.wikipedia.org/wiki/Ishango_bone
2. http://www.math.buffalo.edu/mad/Ancient-Afrika/ishango.html
3. https://www.google.com/search?q=ishango+bone&tbm=isch&tbo=u&source=univ&sa=X&ei=ztRlUrn6JcnS2QXtm4HACQ&sqi=2&ved=0CD0QsAQ&biw=1280&bih=709
4. http://mathworld.wolfram.com/IshangoBone.html
5. https://www.google.com/search?q=ishango+bone&tbm=isch&tbo=u&source=univ&sa=X&ei=ztRlUrn6JcnS2QXtm4HACQ&sqi=2&ved=0CD0QsAQ&biw=1280&bih=709
6. http://primes.utm.edu/glossary/xpage/IshangoBone.html

Afrikans in Virginia Colony of North America
1. http://historyisfun.org/pdf/From-Afrika-to-Virginia/TheAngolanConnection.pdf
2. http://en.wikipedia.org/wiki/Jamestown,_Virginia
3. http://www.virginiaplaces.org/population/slaveorigin.html

4. http://www.nationsencyclopedia.com/Afrika/Angola-HISTORY.html
5. http://www.britannica.com/EBchecked/topic/371373/Mbundu
6. http://en.wikipedia.org/wiki/Ambundu

Development of Caucasians and Maps
1. http://realhistoryww.com/world_history/ancient/White_people.htm
2. http://en.wikipedia.org/wiki/Sundaland

www.ingramcontent.com/pod-product-compliance
Lightning Source LLC
Chambersburg PA
CBHW071119090426
42736CB00012B/1962